∞

The Temperament
God Gave You

The Temperament God Gave You

The Classic Key to Knowing Yourself,
Getting Along with Others,
and Growing Closer to the Lord

by
Art Bennett, LMFT
and
Laraine Bennett

SOPHIA INSTITUTE PRESS®
Manchester, New Hampshire

Sophia Institute Press®
Box 5284, Manchester, NH 03108
1-800-888-9344
www.sophiainstitute.com

Library of Congress Cataloging-in-Publication Data

Bennett, Art.
    The temperament God gave you : the classic key to knowing yourself, getting along with others, and growing closer to the Lord / by Art Bennett and Laraine Bennett.
       p. cm.
    Includes bibliographical references.
    ISBN 1-933184-02-7 (pbk. : alk. paper)
    1. Temperament — Religious aspects — Christianity. I. Bennett, Laraine. II. Title.
    BV4509.5.B447 2005
    233'.5 — dc22   2005006577

05 06 07 08 09 10 9 8 7 6 5 4 3 2

To Pope John Paul II

Contents

∞

Acknowledgments

With deep gratitude we acknowledge Father James Swanson, L.C., who first showed us the relevance of the temperaments to our spiritual and psychological growth; Father Richard Gill, L.C., our beloved (sanguine) spiritual director, who first suggested that we write a book; and Father John Hopkins, L.C., who reminds us that we must never use temperament as a sleight of hand to dodge the realities of actual sin and our need for conversion.

We also thank our (uniquely melancholic-sanguine) editor, Todd Aglialoro, for his faith in this project, for his attention to detail, and for not allowing sanguine Laraine and phlegmatic Art to settle for the first rough draft. We thank all our friends who shared with us their temperament stories and especially our parents, William and Teje Etchemendy and Art and Mildred Bennett. Last, but never least, we are grateful to God for giving us our wonderful children — Lianna, Ray, Sam, and Lucy — who enthusiastically participated in many discussions about temperament and contributed their own stories to our book.

∞

Foreword

You've probably heard the story of the country bumpkin who discovers that every time he leads his horse into the new barn that he has built, the poor horse hits its head on the strut spanning the entrance. One day, he sets his mind to fixing the situation by carving out a six-inch oval of wood from the strut just above where the horse's head passes. As he is getting underway with saw in hand, a friend happens upon him and asks what on earth he's doing, cutting out a section of his barn. The good man explains the horse's predicament. "But," the friend insists, "why don't you just dig out six inches of earth at the entrance to the barn?" Without hesitating, the country bumpkin retorts, "It's not his legs that are the problem; it's his head!"

Sometimes we just miss the obvious — and never is this truer than when it comes to dealing with ourselves! Mood swings, emotional reactions, ups and downs, knee-jerk responses, and apparently incorrigible behavioral ruts are the cause of countless heartaches and frustrations with ourselves and others. We want to know where it all comes from and what we can do about it. We seek answers on the self-help shelf or in the counselor's office, or perhaps at the drugstore. Too often, however, we fail to get to the root of our difficulties. Unwittingly at times, we get caught up in dealing with symptoms, without ever getting to the malady itself. Like our country bumpkin, we waste precious time and energy (and money!) on quasi-solutions and awkward personal strategems to rectify negative behavior while failing to perceive that the real solutions lie elsewhere. That's because the obvious often remains obscure until someone points it out to us.

So, if you are seeking *real* answers to what makes you tick, you've got the right book. And if you are a committed Christian, you've got an added value, because the authors are endeavoring to give you not only the key to keen self-understanding, but also an extraordinary tool for achieving personal holiness — the ultimate solution to the problem of the self!

Laraine and Art Bennett have done us a tremendous service in writing this book. Tapping into their vast experience in counseling, and often illustrating the theory with candid, personal (and humorous) self-disclosures, the authors have made learning about the temperaments — *and how to grow in holiness through our God-given temperament* — easy and fun.

Now, I happen to know something about temperaments, because I've got one myself; I'm a textbook case of the choleric-sanguine. I am also a Catholic priest, a confessor, and a spiritual director. I deal a lot with the human heart (an extraordinary blessing and privilege!). I have seen time and time again just how incomparably valuable an understanding of one's temperament can be for living a genuinely fulfilling (and holy) life. How often, for my spiritual directees, has the point of departure for genuine progress in the spiritual life been to finally come to an understanding of their temperament!

The Temperament God Gave You is for adults — especially those seeking personal holiness. Who should read it? Moms and dads, single persons, consecrated persons, the engaged, the recently married, the married-with-grandchildren, counselors of all stripes (especially marriage counselors and those who counsel the engaged), priests (especially spiritual directors and confessors), as well as psychologists and therapists. All will benefit enormously from a book that is bound to become standard reference point for the study of temperaments.

The book reads quickly. It's chock-full of wisdom and common sense articulated in a user-friendly, entertaining prose. So, it's a great time investment. With a minimum of effort, you will assimilate a wealth of information. Almost every page contains a breakthrough in understanding ourselves and others — and we all know how gratifying that is.

The Temperament God Gave You equips you to smooth out the rough edges of your personality, to become a better communicator with your spouse and your children, and to become a facilitator of harmony amongst family and friends. It will also equip you as never before to cooperate with God's grace in the life-project of your transformation into Christ.

I know you're going to love this book!

May our Lord use every page to help you understand that your temperament is a gift and that he gave it to you for a good reason — so that *in and through that temperament*, you can become a saint!

May God bless you!

Father Thomas Berg, L.C., M.A., Ph.D.
Sacramento, California
Palm Sunday, March 20, 2005

∞

Introduction

"The temperaments . . . isn't that sort of like Catholic astrology?"

This kind of question often surfaces when either of us gives a talk on the four classic temperaments. Yet the concept of temperament is neither pop psychology nor self-help gimmick; in fact, it has a long and venerable tradition within Catholic spirituality and moral theology. Many great spiritual writers — such as St. Francis de Sales, the Very Reverend Adolphe Tanquerey, and contemporary theologian Jordan Aumann, O.P. — discuss the concept of temperament and how it affects the spiritual life.

The concept of the four temperaments — choleric, melancholic, sanguine, and phlegmatic — was originally proposed 350 years before the birth of Christ, to explain differences in personalities according to the "humors," or bodily fluids. And after more than two thousand years of intervening medical and psychological advancement, the concept of temperament itself — and in particular the classic four divisions — is still referenced by contemporary psychologists, educators, and spiritual writers.

Why are we writing about the temperaments, and why should you read our book? Over many years as a professional counselor and speaker on family matters, Art began to realize that there was a place for the study of temperament in contemporary spirituality and psychology. Yet although we found the Christian book market was well stocked with accessible, practical books on temperament for individuals and families, for Catholics the only book dedicated to temperament was a short pamphlet written by Father Conrad Hock in 1934, and reissued by the Pallotine Fathers. It offered just enough tantalizing insight to whet our appetite for a thorough, contemporary — and practical — study of the temperaments specifically for Catholics, a study that would show how temperament affects our individual lives, our families, our marriages and even our spiritual lives. Our book is intended to fill that need.

Man is a mysterious union of body and spirit. The only creature on earth that God wanted for his own sake, he is called to greatness. In the Garden of Eden, man was lord of the world, immortal, gifted with preternatural knowledge and God's own supernatural life. His higher faculties perfectly governed his passions and emotions; that is, his spirit ruled his body. The original unity and harmony — within our own persons as well as with one another and with God — was disrupted by sin. After the Fall, man remains divided against himself, alienated from his fellow man and adrift from God, incapable of overcoming the onslaught of darkness, chaos, and evil. St. Paul would later bemoan the loss of that original harmony: "I do not do the good I want, but I do the evil I do not want" (Rom. 7:19). Consequently, we experience both a "high calling and a deep misery"[1] that can be reconciled only through Christ. "Where sin increased, grace overflowed all the more" (Rom. 5:21); God made Christ to "be sin who did not know sin" so that we might be saved (2 Cor. 5:21).

Man is a mystery to others and to himself. Only in Christ can we discover our true selves and discover that high calling: intimate communion with God. Only in Christ will our lives be renewed and transformed, and so all of creation. "For creation awaits with

---

[1] *Gaudium et Spes*, 13.

eager expectation the revelation of the children of God" (Rom. 8:19). Grace never destroys nature, but perfects it.

This book describes the temperaments — part of our human nature — and how they can influence our personality, our motivations, our lives. It is important to understand how our individual temperament affects us and how best to work with its particular strengths and weaknesses to form ourselves both humanly and spiritually. But it is equally important to remember that temperaments never tell the whole story. Understanding temperament doesn't mean we now have a handy label to slap on our kids and our spouses. Our temperament should never be used as an excuse for bad behavior.

Self-knowledge is a virtue that St. Teresa of Avila said must never be neglected: "Self-knowledge is so important that, even if you were raised right up to the heavens, I should like you never to relax your cultivation of it."[2] Genuine self-knowledge will result in humility — never in complacency. By better understanding ourselves and our loved ones, we will be able to improve ourselves and grow in our spiritual lives, and help our children and spouses to become successful and holy individuals as well. When we understand our temperaments, we can begin to master those inclinations or untoward reactions that may thwart our growth in virtue and in love. We will develop greater compassion for others and will stand ready to encourage and strengthen our loved ones — to begin that transformation of hearts which, through the grace of God, will build a civilization of life and love here on earth and ultimately, intimate friendship with him.

---

[2] St. Teresa of Avila, *Interior Castle*, trans. Allison Peers (New York: Doubleday, 1989), 38.

∞

The Temperament
God Gave You

Chapter 1

∞

What Is Temperament?

"It is native personality, and that alone, that
endows a man to stand before presidents or
generals, or in any distinguish'd collection,
with *aplomb* — and *not* culture, or any
knowledge or intellect whatever."

Walt Whitman

"Grace builds upon nature."

St. Thomas Aquinas

"Know thyself, and thy
faults, and thus live."

St. Augustine

❧

Have you ever wondered why some children seem to have been born neat, while others leave a tornado in their wake? Why are some people always upbeat and optimistic, their glass "half full," while others seem to be enveloped in a black cloud, their glass always "half empty"? For some, no passing thought goes unexpressed, while others need to weigh every word. And why is it that some people view every statement of opinion as a declaration of war, yet others seem to be able to shrug off major insults without skipping a beat?

Quick-tempered or even-keeled? "Strike while the iron is hot" or "Let's wait and see"? Laid-back or prone to flying off the handle? The answer begins with our *temperament*.

We are each born with a basic temperament, which is the *sum of our natural preferences;* it shapes our thoughts, ideas, impressions, and the way we tend to react to our environment and to other people. It is our predisposition to react in certain ways, hardwired in us. It is not learned or acquired through contact with our environment. It is not a product of childhood trauma or repressed memories. In a word, it is "nature," as distinguished from "nurture."

❧

What temperament is not

Temperament is not the same as personality. *Personality* refers to the whole of an individual's patterns of behavior, thoughts, and emotions. In this book, we are considering temperament only,

5

which is but one aspect of an individual's total personality — the aspect related to behavior and reaction.

Within the Catholic tradition, temperament is defined as the pattern of inclinations and reactions that proceed from the physiological constitution of an individual.[3] Our personality may begin with a basic temperament, but it is clearly and significantly affected by environment, education, and free choices. For the purposes of this book, we will refer to the other aspects of personality — the products of environment, upbringing, education, habitual responses, and free choice — as *character*.

Temperament may be viewed as the raw material that an artist uses to create his masterpiece: the stone used in the sculpture may be carved easily or with difficulty; it has a certain color and pattern; it is durable or malleable. Yet the artist uses inspiration, experience, and talent to create a unique sculpture; even if the artist always sculpts in marble, the end product will be unique every time.

So, too, an individual's total personality will be affected by his education, experiences, free choice . . . and grace. The raw material is temperament, but the final creation requires the artist's education, talent, and inspiration.

∞

Can temperament change?

Because our temperament is something we are born with, rather than something we acquire as a result of our upbringing or our free choices in life, it is something that can never be totally

---

[3] Jordan Aumann, O.P., *Spiritual Theology* (Allen, Texas: Christian Classics, 1980), 140; Adolphe Tanquerey, *The Spiritual Life* (Tournai: Desclée and Company, 1930; reprinted by TAN Books), 8 in Appendix.

destroyed. But, it can be shaped and molded. Over time we can even learn to act in ways that are contrary to our temperament; to do the opposite of what "comes naturally."

For example, if I tend to be naturally rather quiet and inclined to solitude, this does not mean that I can't become a good public speaker or behave in an extraverted fashion when the occasion calls for it. When we say that we are "introverted," we mean simply that a more reserved approach to people is our *first* choice; it is our *preference*, our "natural instinct."

So our temperament neither defines our personality completely nor locks us into one pattern of reactions. But it does tell us how we will naturally *tend* to react, and it makes certain behaviors, responses, virtues, and vices easier or more difficult for us.

∾

Know yourself, and others

It's important to remember that, even though temperament is a key part of how we're made and how we will tend to behave, it is not the most critical of all factors influencing our personality, our actions, and thus our eternal destiny. For ultimately our lives will be shaped by how we exercise that fundamental gift from God: our free will. An individual can never be reduced to the sum of his temperament or his environment.

Nonetheless, the study of temperaments is very useful. Understanding our temperament helps deepen our understanding of ourselves and others. We find it easy to turn a blind eye to our own defects and bad habits, making self-knowledge difficult to achieve: "Why do you notice the splinter in your brother's eye, but do not perceive the wooden beam in your own eye?" (Matt. 7:3). When we begin to see ourselves as we truly are, we can begin to make conscious changes for the better.

Understanding temperament also helps us accept, understand, and truly appreciate others. Parents can learn what really motivates a particular child, based on his temperament. Spouses can learn how better to express their love for each other and how to avoid communication deficits that sometimes arise directly from the disparity between temperaments. Teachers will gain empathy for their students, and bosses will learn what can motivate their employees. We will all gain insight into the spiritual difficulties we might face due to our temperament, and can learn new ways to improve our prayer life and grow in holiness.

In short, the four temperaments provide us with a key to unlocking the mystery of our own selves and of our loved ones, and can give us a way to improve all of our relationships by identifying those natural tendencies that can either benefit us or trip us up.

∞

Origin of the temperaments

The tradition that gave us the four "classical" temperaments goes back thousands of years.

Hippocrates (c. 460-377 B.C.), the "father of medical science," may have been the first to develop a personality theory. He claimed that human bodies contained four main types of fluid, and that each individual could be categorized as one of four temperaments based on an imbalance of those fluids in his body — hence, the rather unappealing names:

- *Choleric:* yellow bile from the liver.

- *Sanguine:* blood from the heart.

- *Melancholic:* black bile from the kidneys.

- *Phlegmatic:* phlegm from the lungs.

Around 190 A.D., the Roman physician Galen, following Hippocrates, proposed that the balance of our bodily fluids (the "humors") indeed affects our temperament, but positively, rather than as the result of a negative imbalance. Thus, the "sanguine" temperament was eager and optimistic; the "melancholic" was doleful; "choleric" passionate, and the "phlegmatic" calm.

In *The Republic*, Plato wrote about four kinds of character and their contribution to the social order. Clinical psychologist David Keirsey relates Plato's characters to the original four types of temperament: the *iconic* was "artistic," or sanguine; the *pistic* was the "guardian" or "caretaker" and was melancholic; the *noetic* was an "idealist" and was choleric; and the *dianoetic* character was "rational," a "logical investigator," or phlegmatic.[4]

In the sixteenth century, a Swiss physician and alchemist named Paracelsus compared the four temperament types to the four elements of fire, air, water, and earth. He added the concept of the "fifth element," or "quintessence," which was the mysterious connection and balance among the four elements.

Although the concept of the four types had been around since the early Greeks, the use of the word *temperament* first came into use in the seventeenth century. The Latin word *temperamentum*, or "mixture," was used to refer to the necessary balance that was sought in order to achieve health and well-being.

In 1920, Swiss psychologist Carl Jung advanced the theory that different personality types approached the outside world in distinct manners and could be clearly categorized accordingly.

---

[4] Although temporarily forgotten during the latter part of the nineteenth century, by the early part of the twentieth century there were nearly five thousand reports on the subject (David Keirsey, *Please Understand Me II* [Prometheus Nemesis Book Company, 1978], 25).

The Temperament God Gave You

Isabel Briggs Myers (1897-1979) spent forty years refining the Jungian typology into the *Myers-Briggs Type Indicator*, with its sixteen types of personality. The *Myers-Briggs Type Indicator*, or MBTI, is considered to be one of the most widely used personality inventories available and has achieved great popular success.

Yet David Keirsey, in his *Keirsey Temperament Sorter*, has ascertained (after extensive research into both Jungian typology and the MBTI) that the sixteen types really boil down to — surprise! — *four basic temperaments.*[5]

Keirsey avows that two thousand years of consistency in terms of temperament distinctions is no accident. These distinctions "reflect a fundamental pattern in the warp and woof of the fabric of human nature."[6] The same four basic temperament types have remained largely unchanged (although the terminology may have changed) throughout the centuries.

Each of us is uniquely and predominantly *one* of the temperaments: *choleric, phlegmatic, melancholic,* or *sanguine.* Today, people all over the world are re-discovering the value and wisdom of this most ancient tool for understanding themselves and others.

∽

Making the temperaments work for you

In clinical practice and through many years spent managing programs and people, we have discovered that knowing the differences in temperament really does help improve communication

---

[5] Keirsey, *Please Understand Me II*, 26.

[6] Ibid. Unlike Keirsey, however, we differentiate temperaments according to extravert/introvert and thinking/feeling *preferences* (where *thinking* and *feeling* are understood in terms of whether a person makes decisions based on logic/ideas or on relationships/people).

with spouses, children, and colleagues; it really does helps us understand our own individual strengths and weaknesses.

Putting the temperaments to work begins with self-knowledge. If, for example, I know that I have a very short fuse, I will try to avoid provocations that inevitably make me angry, and I can learn to practice calming techniques. I can, at the same time, try to become more understanding of that peaceful, slow-moving co-worker who drives me nuts.

As a parent, I can become more understanding of differences in my children's temperaments. The thoughtful, dreamy child who seems to be lost in her own thoughts is not deliberately being antisocial, nor was she deprived of appropriate social contacts; it is simply part of her temperament. Understanding her temperament, I can realize that throwing her into a crowd of noisy children will not be the best way to encourage her social skills, and I will instead gently teach her how to develop her conversational abilities.

Each temperament has its own peculiar strengths and weaknesses. We should be aware of and accept them, and also work to capitalize on the strengths and improve the weaknesses. However, we do not seek to understand our temperament simply so that we may have a handy excuse for our own bad behavior. Rather, we want to understand others better, improve our relationships, enlarge our capacity for love, and become more effective in pursuing our goals.

People of certain temperaments, for example, find job interviews particularly challenging. They are tempted to understate their talents and abilities — not because of authentic humility, but rather simply because of a natural tendency to be cautious, introverted, or timid. Knowing yourself in such a situation can help you fight this natural tendency, rather than simply going along with what comes easiest.

The Temperament God Gave You

Parents will discover that some children, because of their temperament, have a natural tendency to overlook details — not because they have attention deficit disorder or because they are misbehaving. Parents can help such children develop awareness of this tendency and develop strategies to overcome it.

An understanding of temperaments can help spouses put to rest some of those ongoing, never-ending arguments: *Why does she always want to go out, just when I am looking forward to a quiet evening at home? Why does he get into such a temper when the house is cluttered? I can't help it if the kids play with toys!* People of some temperaments are driven to distraction by a lack of order. Others thrive on being around people and participating in exciting activities. Still others require a lot of peace and quiet.

If we learn to appreciate certain aspects of our spouse's temperament, we can make sure we aren't unnecessarily "pushing buttons" and can learn to compromise: *Let's go out one night this week, but not right after a rough day at work. I'll get the kids to clean the house before their dad gets home, so he can really relax after work and enjoy his dinner.*

Another common use of temperaments is learning to discover what truly *motivates* others. For example, I might have a temperament that responds well to challenges, such as "Our sales team has achieved only thirty percent of its goal. We need you guys to get out there and turn that around!" However, if my sales staff is composed of phlegmatics and melancholics, I will soon find that everyone is discouraged, depressed, and thinking about quitting. I need to learn to motivate in a different way to build morale.

The temperaments reveal our natural tendencies; they do not seal our fate. Our awareness of our tendencies enables us to make decisions about the best possible response in any given situation, rather than always cruising on automatic pilot. We must learn how to make the appropriate response, given the particular situation, and not just knee-jerk reactions based on our natural preferences. Understanding temperament also helps us in our spiritual lives. A person of one temperament may be particularly given to order and fairness, but might need to work on joyfully encouraging other people. Someone of another temperament may find working in the apostolate something quite easy and natural, but may have to struggle with making time for quiet reflection and a deep prayer life. Still others will discover that their natural inclination is to avoid abnegation and conflict, and may need a good spiritual director or a prayer group to help them make progress and not settle for the "easy life" or become spiritual couch potatoes.

Plato quoted Socrates as saying that the unexamined life is not worth living. Understanding the temperament that God gave us is a key element in that examination process. We must understand ourselves before we can understand others and the world we inhabit. If I know myself — really know who I am, through understanding my strengths, weaknesses, tendencies, desires, and goals — then I have already taken the first step I need to become more productive, satisfied with my relationships, and truly happy.

As St. Thomas Aquinas said, "Grace builds upon nature." Our temperament is part of our nature — a wounded nature, but nonetheless a nature that can be understood and, with God's help, developed. In fact, the greater our self-understanding, the better our ability to control and direct our unruly moods and emotions — thereby increasing our personal freedom. The harmonious and integral development of all the various aspects of our being — both natural and supernatural — will help us lead happier and more productive lives and become more effective in our Christian vocation, and will help propel us more serenely toward our ultimate goal: heaven.

Chapter 2

∽

Overview of the
Four Temperaments

∽

A Quick Self-Test[7]

1. Sirens begin to whirl behind you and you realize that a police car is pulling you over. You think:

❏ His radar gun couldn't possibly be correct. I was hardly going over the speed limit. The cars in front of me were speeding.

❏ Oh, no! I've heard of people getting arrested for this!

❏ Was I driving fast? What's the speed limit on this road, anyway?

❏ Do I have my wallet? And where did I put that car registration?!

2. You are on a silent weekend retreat. Your cell phone rings. What do you do?

❏ You take the call because it might be important. You are confident it won't impact things negatively.

❏ I'm not going to answer. Don't they realize I am on a *silent* retreat? Why are they bothering me? They are so thoughtless!

[7] On page 249 you will find our own Temperament Indicator, a comprehensive self-test that will help you identify your predominant temperament.

❏ You answer on the first ring and start chatting away. After all, you've been silent too long already.

❏ You don't want to disappoint the person on the other end, so you take the call, but you whisper, so no one will hear.

3. Your boss asks you to come into his office. You think:

❏ He has finally recognized my superior contributions. I'm getting a raise!

❏ What's gone wrong *now?* I'll bet that new division manager has gotten caught in one of those boondoggles of his.

❏ He probably likes my idea for the Christmas-party theme.

❏ I hope he doesn't want me to work late tonight. . . . Oh well, I guess I'll have to stay. . . . Sigh.

∞

It's all about patterns of reaction

In each of those three items above, the first response is typical of the choleric temperament, the second melancholic, the third is sanguine, and the fourth phlegmatic. This short, humorous quiz illustrates the fundamental feature of the concept of temperament: people of different temperaments tend to respond to identical stimuli in very different ways. Furthermore, the way each person responds tends to be consistent throughout his life. This consistency or coherence of reaction is due to his temperament.

Temperament is most easily understood in terms of *patterns of reaction* — the manner in which different individuals respond to the same stimuli, whether internal or external. This reaction includes both the speed and duration of reaction time, as well as the intensity of the response. A person may respond quickly or slowly to stimuli. The reaction may last a long time, or it may be quickly forgotten. The reaction may be mild, over-the-top, or anywhere in between. And each individual's pattern of reaction will be clearly identifiable and largely unchanging throughout his life.

For example, when someone cuts in front of you on the freeway, are you instantly irritated, muttering oaths under your breath and shaking your fist at them? Or does it occur to you three exits later that you might have been killed . . . and now you're *really* upset? When you were passed over for a promotion, did you brood about it silently and dwell on it for years? Or did you shrug and say, "Better luck next time"? If you read an interesting article, do you immediately send twenty emails to your friends about the incredible insight you had? When someone asks your opinion, do you need to mull over the question for a long time, waiting until you have completed sufficient research before you weigh in on the subject? Or do you immediately start talking — and hope to discover your opinion as you speak? Does it take you a long time to decide who your friends are, or do you instantly bond with many people?

How quickly do you react when you are praised or chastised, offended or insulted, or feel sympathy or aversion to someone or something? Do you react quickly to perceived offenses? Do you speak or retaliate immediately? Or do you seem to be unable to find the words or take action, even though you're greatly distressed by the offense? Perhaps you are rarely upset by offenses, rarely find yourself angered, and rarely harbor any kind of ill-will; your friends say that you're "easy-going."

In all of these scenarios, your temperament will match up with how you tend to react, how quickly you tend to react, and how intensely you tend to react. Four questions can help determine your temperament from your usual manner of reaction.

∽

Extravert or introvert?

One of the primary distinctions among the temperaments is that between *extraversion* and *introversion*. Generally speaking, an extravert is one who tends to focus on and is comfortable with, the external environment (people and events), whereas an introvert tends to focus on and is more comfortable with his interior world (thoughts and emotions). In this book, *extraversion* indicates a broad range of characteristics including (but not limited to) a certain degree of sustained liveliness, gregariousness, enthusiasm, ease of sociability and interaction with the external world. *Introversion* refers to a tendency to be internally focused, reserved, reflective, less warm, less comfortable socially, and less active.

Note that we use the term *extraversion* in the psychological sense (as opposed to the more common, popular word *extroversion*) to refer to this constellation of characteristics. Specifically, it does not simply mean "outgoing" as opposed to "shy." Many introverts are not shy, although they would prefer to spend a quiet evening at home.

The two temperaments with the quickest reactions, choleric and sanguine, are both also primarily extraverted. They are given primarily to *action*, and express their reactions to experiences or thoughts *outwardly*. They are acutely aware of, and are continually reacting to, what is happening outside of themselves.

Extraverts tend to talk more than they listen, to use expressive gestures and facial expressions, and to overstate or repeat their points. Often, an extravert will begin speaking before he even knows what he thinks about the topic — hoping that, by verbalizing, his thoughts will become clear to him as well as to others.

On the other hand, an introvert — usually of melancholic or phlegmatic temperament — when presented with an idea or an experience, requires time to process the information. Where an extravert processes new information by talking about it, an introvert will need time to reflect on it, to internalize and assimilate the new information.

Our introvert daughter tried to plan out in advance her comments for a college course in which one-third of the grade would be based on class participation. She hated to make what she considered random remarks without sufficient reflection — as extraverts tend to do. We had to convince her that, for the sake of the grade, she was going to have to try to say *some* things off the top of her head.

Introverts tend to be more internally focused, more self-aware; they may at times appear aloof or reserved. *Introverted* is not the same as "shy" in the traditional sense. An introvert may be considered shy as a child, but he can overcome such a label through social maturation. As an adult, he may be capable of being the life of the party — but he will find it emotionally draining and would probably prefer to spend a quiet evening at home. Nonetheless, there are introverts in all manner of highly social, outgoing professions: public speakers, salesmen, and comedians.

The distinguishing feature, therefore, in determining whether you are introverted or extraverted is not whether you are considered shy, but whether you tend to respond *internally* and *passively* to stimuli, or (as extraverts do) *outwardly* and *actively*. Do you express yourself easily (extraverted) or with some difficulty (introverted)? Do you have an intense inner life (introverted), or do you look externally for value (extraverted)? Are you tempted to resolve conflicts by talking about them (extravert), or do you tend to internalize conflict and rehearse dialogues inside your head (introvert)? Do you find yourself *energized* and *refreshed* by social interaction (extraverted), or do you find yourself *exhausted* by intense social interaction? Do others consider you *warm* and *friendly*, or do they say that you are *reserved* or *slow to warm up*?

∽

Think first? Or act first?

A motto of the extravert might be: "Act first, think later" (or "Talk first, think later"), while the introvert's motto would be: "Think first, act later." Extraverts will tend to express their thoughts and their feelings immediately, without deep reflection. When a decision has to be made, an extravert will not hesitate either to make his opinions known (cholerics) or seek others' opinions (sanguines). Cholerics and sanguines have little compunction about sharing their thoughts (cholerics) or their feelings (sanguines). Many a mother has moaned about her sanguine child that "no feeling goes unexpressed." Many a friend or co-worker can attest to the choleric's tendency to "shoot from the hip." Cholerics and sanguines feel quite comfortable in front of people at parties, although the choleric may require more "alone time" than the sanguine.

The introverted melancholic will experience greater ease than the phlegmatic in expressing his thoughts and ideas, but will often be regarded as impersonal, demanding, or even cold by acquaintances. The melancholic will not readily reveal his feelings, and he can misread social cues. The introverted phlegmatic, on the other hand, is more attuned to his own feelings as well as to those around him, and cares deeply about others; nonetheless he tends to be reserved and even self-effacing when expressing himself to avoid conflict or out of fear of being hurt. Where the logical and analytical melancholic is comfortable examining and exploring his own thoughts, the inner life of the phlegmatic can sometimes be such a complex puzzle that even he does not want to spend much time analyzing it.

Introverts — whether phlegmatic or melancholic — might at times be accused of being snobby or standoffish in social situations, when, in reality, they simply need time and space to process information and reflect on it (melancholic) or feel comfortable and trusting (phlegmatic). Outward expressions of sociability — smiling, looking others in the eye — which come so easily to sanguines or cholerics, are behaviors that must be learned by people with introverted temperaments. Both melancholics and phlegmatics, because of their tendency to introversion, tend to be somewhat less active or productive externally than the choleric and sanguine temperaments. In general, introverts are more reflective, less confrontational, and less initiating.

∞

Principles or people?

The two temperaments that place the highest value on harmony in relationships, on collaborating with people, and on the importance of taking other people's needs and feelings into account are the sanguine and the phlegmatic. Are you a good collaborator and a team player? Do you feel uncomfortable when there is conflict or disagreement? Do you sometimes overextend yourself in trying to help others? Are you good at putting yourself in someone else's shoes? Then you may be sanguine (if you are extraverted) or phlegmatic (if you are introverted).

The sanguine is your classic "people person," combining extraversion with a natural desire to please people and form relationships. The phlegmatic is also relationship-oriented, although in an introverted way. Phlegmatics want everyone around them to be happy; they want to avoid and dispel conflict. The sanguine and phlegmatic temperaments place a high priority on getting along, so they tend to be adaptable and cooperative — provided their most fundamental needs have been met. To preserve harmony, both will tend to agree with those around them, rather than try to impose their own will or try to take charge.

Cholerics and melancholics, on the other hand, generally do not make decisions based on pleasing others or on maintaining peaceful relationships. Rather, they are motivated by their goals, their ideas, and their ideals. They do not value feelings or sentiments as much as they value principles. They tend to seek objectivity and clarity in a given situation or decision, rather than being concerned with how people are affected by it or feel about it. If forced to choose between being truthful or being tactful, the cholerics and melancholics will choose *truth*.

Now ask yourself:

❑ Am I extraverted or introverted?

❑ Do I make decisions based primarily on logical principles or on relationships?

∞

Leadership comes in all types

The two temperament types with the greatest intensity of reaction and the longest duration of reaction — the choleric and the melancholic — are also the two classic "leader" types. Although someone of any of the four temperaments can develop strong leadership skills, the choleric and melancholics are naturally leaders, because they tend to want to do things their own way. On the downside, they can have difficulty taking direction when necessary and will sometimes try not merely to lead others, but to control them. The choleric will exercise control in an open, overt way, whereas the melancholic tends to control quietly behind the scenes.

Overview of the Four Temperaments

The choleric loves to take charge of projects and people, and may rush ahead without consultation or reflection. The melancholic takes a more back-seat approach; rather than initiate, he analyzes. While the choleric makes the battle plans and rallies the troops, the melancholic determines where the project falls short of the ideal. A choleric-melancholic planning committee would be an excellent pairing: the choleric would kick-start the program and come up with the initial strategy, and the melancholic would be the devil's advocate, correcting any hasty errors and perfecting the plan.

The choleric tends to be outspoken and headstrong, argumentative and questioning. The melancholic will not be quick to speak his mind, but will make critical judgments internally. Teachers will have to work to win the respect of both cholerics and melancholics. Cholerics begin with the presumption that everyone else is less intelligent than they are. Melancholics cannot help but note imperfections in themselves and others. Presentations of ideas will be met with criticism by both — the choleric's verbal and the melancholic's unspoken.

Sanguines and phlegmatics are often more comfortable in a team and often prefer to take a back-seat or supportive role. They do not usually feel comfortable taking on the often arduous and demanding tasks that leadership entails — making unpopular decisions for the sake of the mission, taking charge and delegating, staying on task and holding others to theirs, and so forth. Nonetheless, when they put their mind to it, they often make the best leaders. They will use their ability to understand and connect with people to become *servant-leaders* (phlegmatics) who lead by doing as much as — or more than — they ask of others or *charismatic* leaders (sanguines), who lead on the force of their enthusiasm and personality.

In the next chapter, we will discuss in detail the four classic temperaments. We recommend that you view this study of temperaments as a tool for self-assessment and an aid to understanding and appreciating others. Do not imagine that each person must fit exactly into one of these four boxes. Rather, view these portraits of the four temperaments as a key to understanding those *tendencies* which, deriving from our nature, influence our total personality.

Chapter 3

∽

Which Temperament Is Mine?

"Every temperament is in itself good,
and with each one man can do
good and work out his salvation."

Father Conrad Hock

∽

Let's now take a quick snapshot of each of the four classic temperaments: choleric, melancholic, sanguine, and phlegmatic. Remember: these snapshots represent the "pure ideal" of the temperament
and that most people will not find themselves pictured exactly.
Most people will have a combination of two temperaments, with
one dominating (see chapter 9 for a complete discussion of primary and secondary temperaments).

THE CHOLERIC

*"Do you not know that the runners in the
stadium all run in the race, but only one wins
the prize? Run so as to win"* (1 Cor. 9:24).

Enthusiasm, energy, intelligence, and a strong will combine to make the choleric temperament a classic go-getter. Whether at home or on the job, the choleric will take charge and get many things accomplished in a short time. The choleric reacts quickly and intensely; decisiveness is his hallmark. In addition, he is extraverted and self-confident, comfortable taking charge of people as well as situations. Opposition is never a stumbling block, but rather, a further incentive to action. Dynamic and direct, the choleric has a keen mind and thinks independently. He will always let you know what he's thinking.

The choleric's enthusiasm and energy will attract others to him. He thrives on activity; work invigorates him. He is optimistic and magnanimous; he values success in his endeavors and sets high goals. He is comfortable with power, blossoms in competition, and is confident in his decisions.

Cholerics are eminently rational; they expect to hear good reasons for any argument. Even as children, they will not accept "Because I said so" as sufficient reason for doing something. Cholerics can grasp the big picture and can communicate the vision to others; they are natural organizers and tend to rise to positions of authority. They easily express their ideas to others, but are less willing to listen. They hate to "waste time" on meetings, employee relations, or small details. Many entrepreneurs are cholerics. They tend not to delegate because they believe that they can do it better and faster themselves and because they enjoy their own productivity. A choleric can also be successful as a CEO, a military leader, a founder, or in any other profession where his leadership and vision is valued.

There is, of course, a downside to this driven and intense personality. The choleric is quick to judge, to form an opinion, and to charge ahead stubbornly — often without proper reflection and at times without compassion for people in his way. If you have ever brought home something that has to be assembled, and plunged right in without looking at the instructions, you may be a choleric. A choleric thinks that reading directions or studying a map before heading out the door is a waste of time; he can figure it out on the way.

His intelligence, decisiveness, and high productivity make the choleric impatient with — sometimes even contemptuous of — those who are less talented. He can be domineering, obstinate, dictatorial, overly ambitious, and hardhearted. He is prone to pride and anger. Father Conrad Hock writes, "The choleric prefers to die rather than to humble himself."[8] Sometimes it can seem as though people are a secondary consideration to the choleric. A choleric who is not trying to grow in virtue can quickly become utilitarian in his approach.

If you are choleric, do not be offended by the fact that many of the infamous dictators of history shared your temperament. Cholerics tend to lead with the strength of an idea, a goal, or sheer enthusiasm, rather than taking the time to mold, convince, or teach the people they are leading. It is equally true that many great saints are of this temperament. St. Paul was once the greatest persecutor of the Christians; after his conversion, he became the most dynamic apostle.

---

[8] Rev. Conrad Hock, *The Four Temperaments*, rev. ed. (Milwaukee: The Pallotine Fathers, Inc., 1962), 20.

The choleric may fear intimacy in personal relationships; he is too independent, impatient, and insensitive. He can be rash and imprudent when making decisions, and then deny that he has made an error. He tends to hide his insecurities while blaming others for his own mistakes.

Cholerics will be valuable employees — if not the founder of the business itself. They are self-motivated, task-oriented, quick-thinking, pragmatic, and energetic. They enjoy their work. They enjoy leading projects and people, but sometimes need to be reminded that not everyone works as quickly as they do. Sometimes, in their determination to achieve results, they can roll over their co-workers' feelings to accomplish the task at hand.

A spiritual life marked by strict discipline and obedience is critical for the choleric, to help him overcome his tendencies to pride, anger, and obstinacy. He will need to develop compassion, humility, tenderness, and understanding in dealing with others. But it will be first necessary to convince the choleric that he *needs* the spiritual life, that he can *trust* a spiritual director, that he must humble himself before God and learn the virtue of obedience. He will learn to be more understanding and forgiving of his fellow man and will develop greater humility when he realizes that the natural gifts of his temperament are gifts from God and are not something he personally earned or deserved.

THE MELANCHOLIC
Blessed are they who hunger and
thirst for righteousness (Matt. 5:6).

The melancholic, more than any other temperament, tends to value the *ideal* — whether it be truth, beauty, or justice, and all that is noble. He can be thoughtful, pious, and compassionate, given to solitude and reflection. It is said that the melancholic so longs for heaven that everything on earth falls short. Sensitive and idealistic, he is deeply concerned about injustice and vice. His idealism combined with compassion for humanity and passion for justice may lead him to a humanitarian vocation. Great writers, poets, artists, and composers have been of this temperament.

Many melancholics have become great saints — founders of religious orders, reformers, great mystics and theologians. The melancholic is principled, consistent, faithful, and persevering. He is orderly, diligent, and attentive to detail. He appreciates the mystery and depth of life.

But that same idealism of melancholics can also cause them to become critical or judgmental of others who don't "measure up." This idealism lends itself to leadership skills, or sometimes causes melancholics to be impractical and intractable, not team players. They are skeptical about what may appear to be simplistic labels and categories — such as the four temperaments.

The melancholic temperament is characterized by a weak or dull initial reaction to stimuli, followed by an increase in intensity over time; the reaction then tends to last a long time. Because of their slowness to react and their tendency to introversion, melancholics base much of their decision-making on ideals. They long for perfection, yet so few people can meet their expectations and their dreams. No wonder they often have their nose in a book!

Melancholics form relationships very slowly; in fact, they're usually quite content to be left alone. They do not initiate relationships, and it may take a long time for them really to trust. But when they do form a relationship, they will be faithful and true to a fault. Yet if their trust is violated, and they become aware of the betrayal, they can be relentless in unforgiveness.

The melancholic's reflective nature, combined with his goal of reaching perfection, will cause him to note all the difficulties of a new venture or a proposed project, worry about all the possible negative outcomes, and pinpoint errors and injustices. The effect can paralyze the melancholic. When Hamlet uttered his famous "To be, or not to be" soliloquy, he was expressing a fundamental melancholic disposition. Hamlet was unable to act, due to his intense introspection and its stultifying effect.

The melancholic longs for perfection and, failing to achieve that, may begin to lack self-confidence and become despondent. He sees problems where other temperaments (such as the choleric) see challenges or opportunities. Ironically, however, although small details can stump them, melancholics can often handle the truly big crises with grace and aplomb.

Why do melancholics sweat the small stuff, but not the big stuff? We are not sure what the answer is to this conundrum of the very complex melancholic temperament. One theory is that the melancholic lives his daily life with the expectation that, any minute, the "other shoe will drop."

One melancholic we know always has a list of complaints ready: the kids are misbehaving, the job market looks grim, the in-laws are warring. But when serious illness threatened the family, this melancholic was calm under the pressure and drew upon spiritual strength. Without such a foundation, though, the melancholic could just as easily sink into depression.

Because of their tendency to reflect on and to weigh every pro and con, melancholics can appear to be irresolute and indecisive. They may spend too much time on planning and preparing, and too little time putting their plans into action. It is sometimes very difficult for them to bring others aboard a project because they don't know how to convey enthusiasm for it — not because they lack that enthusiasm inside themselves. For some reason, melancholics tend to be less physically vigorous than other temperaments. Where a choleric seems to abound in energetic enthusiasm, the melancholic tends to be quieter, weaker, and more prone to small illnesses that sap his will.

Because of their introversion and their tendency to pessimism, melancholics can become excessively self-absorbed. They should fight to achieve self-confidence and to place their trust in God. They need to strive to become attentive and generous to others in need (fighting against the temptation to self-pity). Self-pity is a trap that can keep the melancholic in a myopic, unproductive lifestyle. Teachers and parents can help their melancholic students and children by encouraging them to exercise regularly and to eat well and to learn to develop confidence, optimism, and enthusiasm.

Sometimes the first step is the most difficult. Because of his acute sense of what can go wrong, a melancholic will often exhibit a notable indecisiveness at the beginning of a project or new stage of life. The melancholic needs to be helped over this hump, perhaps by an understanding teacher or parent or spiritual director who can help give him the confidence he lacks and inspire him with optimism.

As Father Hock puts it, the melancholic has a "strong will coupled with talent and power," but he can be overly cautious to the point that he has "no courage." "It has become proverbial therefore: 'Throw the melancholic into the water, and he will learn to swim.' "[9]

On the job, someone whose primary temperament is melancholic will be a great asset in any work requiring precision, detail, consistency, organization, and in-depth analysis. We know several melancholics who are editors, writers, educators, and financial analysts. Some are even your classic "watch dogs," sniffing out corporate shenanigans. Just don't ask them to make sales calls! Also, don't expect them to be the most sensitive people-managers: melancholics can overlook necessary relational, team-building, and motivational aspects of dealing with people.

In his spiritual life, the melancholic should focus on personal intimacy with Christ, because his nature is drawn to the highest of ideals and will never rest until, as St. Augustine said, it rests in the Lord. Furthermore, only through an intimate relationship with Christ will the melancholic learn to temper his overly critical expectations of other people — such trust should be placed in God alone — and to overcome his natural tendency to sadness.

A strong interior life will help the melancholic attain intimacy with God, supernatural joy and peace. A good spiritual director can greatly help the melancholic by helping him set prudential goals, remind him to take care of his health and human needs, and to develop definitive spiritual resolutions. (See chapter 10 for more on the spiritual life.)

[9] Ibid., 37.

THE SANGUINE
"God loves a cheerful giver" *(2 Cor. 9:7).*

The creative, fun-loving, high-spirited sanguine's natural tendency to look on the bright side, to enjoy people, and to seek out adventure sometimes results in a label of superficiality and frivolity. But the world is a brighter, more joyful place because of the inspiration, enthusiasm, and fellowship he provides.

A strength of the sanguine is his ability to "live in the present moment"; because he does not dwell on the past, nor spend time worrying about the future, he has a very optimistic, joyful attitude toward life. The sanguine is often adventuresome, enterprising, and creative — and is a source of inspiration to others.

Although quickly and easily aroused to emotion or reaction, the sanguine does not retain the reaction for any length of time. His curiosity is easily piqued and his interest easily aroused; combined with his natural extraversion, this makes the sanguine typically friendly, outgoing, and communicative, always on the lookout for new adventures and new friends. He is very attuned to his five senses, which gives him a good eye for detail and attention to appearance. (This can also be a source of trouble, if he becomes overly drawn to sensible pleasures and external attractions.)

Relationships are extremely important to sanguines; they are warmhearted, compassionate, generous, and eager to please. They are energized by large groups, and cooperative with and accepting of others. They want to please their parents and teachers.

Sanguines' eagerness to please is, however, sometimes at odds with their love of the limelight. Our sanguine son has received quite a few detentions (undeserved, he believes) for his attention-getting antics in the classroom. Sanguines love to be the center of attention, and they prefer quantity (not necessarily quality) of friendships. They want to make others happy — or at least get a big laugh!

The mercurial sanguine wears his emotions on his sleeve, although these emotions are not long-lived and might be given to rashness, imprudence, and impulsivity. (He is rarely willfully defiant or obstinate.) The sanguine child learns quickly, although he might have difficulty memorizing. Continually discovering some new interest, like butterflies flitting from flower to flower, sanguines can find it difficult to attain great depth in one area of study. It is not that they do not have the intellectual capacity, but rather that their attention is so easily captured by something new.

Weaknesses of the sanguine temperament include the tendency toward superficiality (due to the immediacy of their reactions and their creative imaginations), inconstancy (due to the short duration of their impressions), and sensuality (lacking the perseverance to withstand temptation once their passions are aroused). Because he places such a high value on relationships and pleasing others, a sanguine is often tempted to forsake what he knows is right in order to fit in with the crowd.

It is sometimes said that sanguines "enter the room mouth-first." Their love of the limelight makes them prone to exaggeration and rash words, and to teasing others. Their tendency to talk before they think often results in having to apologize for hurting someone's feelings. Making such an apology is not usually difficult for the sanguine, who really wants everyone to love him. Spiritual writers point out that going to Confession is not difficult for the sanguine; whereas the choleric does not want to confess his sins out of pride, and the melancholic finds it extremely painful to reveal his deeply hidden faults.

The sanguine is likely to enjoy an occupation that highlights dealing with people. He will want to use his quick-thinking creativity to come up with new ideas, projects, and ventures. Detailed, arduous tasks that require working independently, on the other hand, may be more of a struggle for the enthusiastic, sociable sanguine.

In the spiritual life, the sanguine is less likely to fall prey to a pharisaical legalism because he prioritizes relationships and freedom of expression. But, when poorly formed in the Faith, this tendency can lead to an undisciplined and incoherent set of beliefs based on personal preferences rather than on the truth. If, however, the sanguine develops a close personal relationship with Christ, he can develop faithfulness and obedience to authentic Church teaching. "If you love me, you will keep my commandments" (John 14:15).

When the life-loving, people-pleasing sanguine discovers that Jesus Christ is the true friend of his soul, he embarks on a journey toward spiritual maturity; depth and constancy of personality will result. Such a journey will help him discover who he truly is — and who is the One who is most important to please!

Sanguines should be highly valued members of a family, organization, or religious community: they are self-giving, generous, cooperative, and loving. When motivated by a love for Christ and with attention to spiritual formation, the sanguine will exhibit great energy, sensitivity, and vivacity in spreading the Kingdom and bringing more souls to Christ.

The Temperament God Gave You

THE PHLEGMATIC
Blessed are the peacemakers, for they
will be called children of God (Matt. 5:9).

Phlegmatics are reserved, prudent, sensible, reflective, respectful, and dependable. They are not easily insulted or provoked to
anger, nor are they given to exuberance or exaggeration in speech.
They are loyal and committed, tolerant and supportive. They possess a hidden will of iron that is often overlooked, because they are
such agreeable people. They have a knack for diffusing tense situations. Phlegmatics make superb diplomats and military strategists.
They also make excellent firefighters, police officers, and military
officers; they excel in professions where being calm under pressure
is key.

The good news is, if you are of a phlegmatic temperament, you
will not have to attend anger-management courses! It takes a lot to
rile a phlegmatic. They are known for their easy-going nature.
They possess a great deal of common sense and mental balance.
They tend to be clear, concise, and thoughtful in speech and writing. They are excellent listeners and have great empathy for others.
They are supportive friends, patient with difficult people and situations, and considerate at all times. They are accepting of traditions and rules, and will not "buck the system"; they can handle a
bureaucratic system or one that has a clearly delineated hierarchy.

They do not, however, like conflict or confrontation. Our oldest son, a phlegmatic, was recently required to enter a debate
contest at school. What would a peaceful, non-confrontational
phlegmatic do when his grade depended on arguing with an opponent? The result was almost comical. His opponent began, "I believe the drinking age should be twenty-one, because anyone
younger than that would be irresponsible." Our son replied, "I

agree with you, but I think the age should be raised to twenty-two. They are even more responsible." His poor opponent was struck speechless.

On the job, phlegmatics are dependable, punctual, and orderly; they can bring harmony to almost any group. Their introversion, combined with the importance they place on relationships, attracts them to abstract goals such as love, patriotism, religion, and loyalty. They are, however, "reluctant" leaders. They prefer a job with security rather than one that is demanding and high-achieving. Many phlegmatics become teachers: the routine and security of the job appeal to them, and they are well equipped with the patience to deal with kids. Engineering, science, mechanics, and carpentry are also good fields for detail-oriented phlegmatics. In the religious life, it has been suggested that the monks who painstakingly produced the illuminated manuscripts were phlegmatic.

Because of their reserved natures, phlegmatics are sometimes accused of being unassertive, or of lacking enthusiasm and spontaneity. Since they aim to please, and want to avoid conflict at all costs, they may become overly conciliatory. Sometimes they are so conciliatory that it appears they do not even know what their own desires are! Unlike the sanguine, who is characterized by his attraction to things (people, experiences, novelties, and material objects), the phlegmatic is known for avoiding things: conflict among people, or demanding physical labor or mental exertion. The phlegmatic might defer to peer pressure in order to keep the peace or to avoid conflict (and thus, can become overwhelmed), while the sanguine gravitates naturally into the thick of his peer group.

Where the choleric needs to restrain himself, the phlegmatic (whose temperament is diametrically opposed to the choleric's) needs to *arouse* himself. The choleric is passionate; the phlegmatic is dispassionate. Their detachment may appear to signal a lack of interest. A phlegmatic will exhibit this direct, scientific, dispassionate, and realistic approach to his work and his studies. Those who are intellectually gifted can become great scholars and scientists whose analyses are objective, unclouded by the passions of either a sanguine or choleric temperament (likely to jump to conclusions or to pursue their own agenda). Such detachment can be beneficial in scholarly work — allowing phlegmatics to spend countless hours sifting through and analyzing research, for example — but frustrating in a relationship. Once the phlegmatic is aroused, however, to achieve a goal or pursue an ideal, he will be constant and persevering.

In the spiritual life, a phlegmatic may find it much easier to accept doctrines and teachings of the Church, and may not be as inclined (as perhaps a choleric might) to argue with the Magisterium. The dutiful and cooperative phlegmatic may take at face value the teachings of the Church and may need to be encouraged to internalize and personalize his faith. A good relationship with his pastor, youth minister, or even a spiritual director will help encourage the phlegmatic to take an *active* role in the apostolate of the Church. If the phlegmatic does not perceive the vital necessity of his own personal contribution, he may end up simply warming the pews on Sunday and never truly embracing his baptismal commitment to help spread the Kingdom of God.

Which Temperament Is Mine?

What if I can't figure out my temperament?

When giving presentations on the temperaments, we have heard the question: "What if I can't figure out what my temperament is?" Usually, after a little probing, we can weed out factors such as job-related tendencies or wished-for personality characteristics, and can ascertain a person's basic, natural temperament.

However, there are other factors that may make it truly difficult to identify your own temperament: for example, a lack of self-knowledge, habitual sin, mental illness, or a dysfunctional upbringing. A job that demands that you act in a way different from your natural temperament also may make it more difficult to identify (although people tend not to last long in such jobs).

Traits acquired through long-term application of the will can also make finding your true temperament tricky. For example, when you first meet our friend John, you will immediately notice his outgoing personality, his friendliness, and his big, hearty laugh. You may thus assume he is sanguine. However, when you get to know him, you will discover that he was actually very quiet and shy as a child and simply decided one day that he was going to change. He worked hard to become skillful at social interactions, and to this day it doesn't come easy. Our friend is very productive and happy in his career as an engineer; but to ask that he become, for example, a salesman, might be asking too much.

Habitual sin can also cause you to exhibit characteristics that may not be related to your temperament, but are, instead, the result of sin. For example, a phlegmatic (who is typically quite easy-going and cooperative) may become angry, argumentative, and mean-spirited as a result of a habit of drinking to excess. Or, a sanguine (who is naturally very open and friendly) may become deceitful and secretive if he is trying to hide an adulterous affair.

Another factor that can cloud a person's temperament is lack of self-knowledge. This can be further complicated when a person is very immature or wants to impress someone else; in such cases, he might mistakenly believe himself — or naively wish — to be of a particular temperament.

Mental illness or psychological damage can also stand in the way of identifying temperament. Now, no one is perfect. Nonetheless, some individuals are more wounded in their human nature than others. People may be afflicted by physical evil, evil arising from sin or moral weakness, diabolical evil, or the pathology arising from mental illness. A severely dysfunctional family of origin can leave deep psychological wounds. Emotional or physical abuse, ignorance, or family members who are mentally ill can cause a young child to grow up internalizing fear and self-hatred — two destructive attitudes that inhibit him from being able to love others, to be trustful and generous, and to love God. Mental illness can severely affect an individual's ability to perceive reality correctly, to make healthy decisions and have healthy relationships, and even to grow spiritually.

Yet God never abandons anyone. He provides all the means necessary for each person's salvation. "I sought whence evil comes, and there was no solution," wrote St. Augustine in his *Confessions*. Yet, through faith we believe that God allows evil only in order to draw from it a greater good. "Where sin increased, grace abounded all the more" (Rom. 5:20).

∞

Spiritual progress may mask temperament
A final and somewhat different kind of factor is growth in holiness, when a person has grown so close to Christ that he exhibits only few (if any) of the weaknesses of his particular temperament.

Which Temperament Is Mine?

St. Ignatius of Loyola was considered to be passionately choleric, yet became so meek and so humble that people who just met him thought he was phlegmatic. St. Thérèse of Lisieux had been a lively, impulsive, strong-willed child, yet many of the sisters who lived with her never guessed what heroic struggles lay hidden beneath her gentle, humble mien.[10] St. Teresa Benedicta of the Cross (Edith Stein) had been precocious, temperamental, and introverted as a young child, and as a young woman suffered severe depression. She later became a brilliant philosopher, writer, lecturer, and Carmelite who wrote, "To suffer and to be happy although suffering, to have one's feet on the earth, to walk on the dirty and rough paths of this earth and yet to be enthroned with Christ at the Father's right hand, to laugh and cry with the children of this world and ceaselessly sing the praises of God with the choirs of angels — this is the life of the Christian until the morning of eternity breaks forth."[11] A melancholic saint is one who exhibits such joy in the Cross.

As you progress in the spiritual life, becoming more Christlike, you, too, may find the characteristic weaknesses of your temperament obscured; and you may through prayer and perseverance develop virtues that are not characteristic. You may come to say, like St. Paul, "Yet I live, no longer I, but Christ lives in me" (Gal. 2:20).

[10]"Many of the nuns thought of [St. Thérèse] as a nice little thing — nothing more. Yet her nature was a violent one. Her mother said of her, 'She flings herself into the most dreadful rages when things don't go as she wants them' " (*The Autobiography of Saint Thérèse of Lisieux: The Story of a Soul*, trans. John Beevers [New York: Doubleday, 1957], 13).

[11]*Love of the Cross.*

∞

We have highlighted each temperament's typical responses and preferences. Bear in mind that these portraits of the temperaments are not set in stone, nor do they seal a person's fate. However, the tendencies noted above can serve as a useful tool for self-analysis and, ultimately, improvement and self-formation.

In the next chapter, we will look at the choleric, the melancholic, the sanguine and the phlegmatic *spouse*; how the temperaments interact with one another, some land mines to avoid, and some useful tips for promoting healthy, positive, loving communication between spouses, which will in turn build healthier, happier marriages.

Chapter 4

∞

Understanding Your Spouse's Temperament

"Between you two there must come sometime
Peace . . . though you be not of one temperament,
Causing each day such violent dissent."

Geoffrey Chaucer

"Nearly all marriages, even happy ones, are
mistakes: in the sense that almost certainly (in
a more perfect world, or even with a little more
care in this very imperfect one) both partners
might be found more suitable mates. But the real
soul-mate is the one you are actually married to."

J.R.R. Tolkien

"Politics doesn't make strange bedfellows —
marriage does."

Groucho Marx

∞

Kate and Ed came into counseling seeking help for their oldest child. They soon realized that there were underlying marital issues that needed to be addressed.[12] Ed tended to avoid conflict and difficult parenting decisions, while Kate felt increasingly burdened by her sense that she was the only disciplinarian in the house. Kate felt that Ed needed to be firmer with their oldest child, yet her nagging and complaining had no effect. Ed, on the other hand, did not agree that their child was deserving of severe punishment, but because he didn't want to start an argument, he simply retreated into silence and inaction.

It was a vicious cycle. The more Kate complained and criticized, the more Ed felt inadequate and retreated into his shell, which, in turn, caused Kate to complain and criticize all the more. Complaints and criticism soon developed into contempt and defensiveness.

Many happily married couples argue and express anger on occasion without causing damage to their relationship. This is part of healthy communication. But anger accompanied by contempt, criticism, defensiveness, and stonewalling can be devastating to a marriage.[13]

---

[12] Although there were genuine concerns regarding the child, there was also a deeper, underlying conflict between the spouses. Parents will often unite temporarily over the child's behavior, effectively alleviating a greater anxiety associated with parental fighting.

[13] John Gottman, Ph.D., *Why Marriages Succeed or Fail* (New York: Simon and Schuster, 1994), 58.

The Temperament God Gave You

Understanding temperament can help couples avoid the damaging effects of poor communication. Spouses usually don't consciously intend to criticize, become defensive, or show contempt for each other. Rather, they fall into habits of negative interactions when they fail to understand and appreciate differences in temperament. When they step out of their habitual patterns of poor communication and learn new ways of communicating, they discover that their spouse, in turn, reacts more positively and lovingly.

Kate, a melancholic-choleric, had been trying to motivate Ed by using strategies that would have worked with her own temperament. She challenged Ed to take charge with the oldest child and listed the many problems she had with her child's behavior. Ed, a peaceful phlegmatic, wasn't motivated by challenges, especially when accompanied by criticism (of himself or his son). In fact, they caused him to become discouraged and to withdraw.

Kate had always been a problem-solver: if there was an injustice to set right, she would defend the innocent; if finances were threatening, she would crunch numbers and analyze worst-case scenarios until she had worked her way into the black. But her phlegmatic husband did not respond to the crisis/challenge model and retreated further and further into his shell, feeling incompetent and helpless. Becoming increasingly discouraged, he simply withdrew and deferred to her authority in matters of discipline. Kate saw this as Ed shirking his fatherly duty and began to criticize more and more. Soon, Ed began to think that maybe the marriage would not work out, because she was "never satisfied," and her expectations were far beyond what he felt capable of.

Because both Kate and Ed are introverts, they did not deal straightforwardly with their issues: both dealt with their feelings indirectly. Kate expressed herself, in a typical melancholic way, in terms of "oughts" and "shoulds," while Ed didn't express himself at all if there was potential for conflict. His phlegmatic, introverted nature led him to prefer silence to debating or taking charge. Motivating and persuading did not come naturally to melancholic Kate, who valued order and justice above relationship-building. As a phlegmatic, Ed wanted to preserve harmonious relationships among all the family members, and he feared that taking a leadership role would cause strife.

Such temperamental differences are often seen as charming — even exciting — in the early days of courtship and marriage. She may be a bit of a worrier, but this has always made him feel protective of her. He is very easy-going and considerate, and this calms her fears. He is inspired by her sense of the ideal, and she appreciates his even-keeled personality. But as the years go by, and challenges in career, child-rearing, and intimacy mount, she finds herself harping on problems in an accusatory way, because he is too passive. He becomes defensive and withdrawn. She assumes her criticisms or challenges are motivating; he hopes that if he withdraws, she will stop.

∞

The gift of self

Many couples are like Kate and Ed. They come into marriage counseling mired in a pattern of nagging, avoiding, criticizing, and stonewalling, and it seems that they have lost the original love and high ideals they once had. How can couples avoid losing that original passion and love for each other? If they are in a rut, how can they regain their sense of intimacy and appreciation for each other? Marriage is meant to be an intimate communion of persons — like the Blessed Trinity itself, a model of self-revelation, forgiveness, and life-giving love. But how can ordinary couples reach such a lofty ideal?

The Temperament God Gave You

The key is what Pope John Paul II calls self-giving love:[14] looking first to what the *other person* needs, rather than focusing on yourself. If you meet your spouse's critical emotional needs, he or she will feel loved, and will, in turn, be much more likely to respond lovingly and positively. When Kate and Ed began to understand and appreciate the differences in their temperaments, they realized that Kate's natural, temperamental way of motivating herself (dwelling on the negative), simply had the opposite effect on Ed, who needed lots of positive encouragement, praise, and respect for his constant, dedicated service to his family. Kate learned to remind herself that "things are not as bad as they seem," when confronted by her son's behavior, reminding herself that he was, after all, just a child. She learned to lead with positive, encouraging comments about Ed's projects and to restrict her critical thoughts. Ed learned that taking a strong leadership role in his family would not *cause* conflict; it would, on the contrary, dispel it. Kate saw the value of Ed's position as peacemaker in the family, and Ed began to take a leadership role in the disciplining of his children, and expressed his appreciation for Kate's involvement with and concern for the kids. They began to communicate with each other more positively, and their marriage was strengthened.

∞

The importance of appreciation

As you will discover as you read our overviews of each temperament, showing appreciation is critical to meeting your spouse's

[14]The sincere gift of self, especially in marriage, is discussed beautifully in John Paul II's 1994 *Letter to Families* and in *Familiaris Consortio,* among other places. Of course, marriages must be rooted first in Christ, in his love and grace.

emotional needs. Appreciation is often expressed through attentiveness, which is so important that John Paul II quotes St. Ambrose adjuring husbands to "reciprocate [your wife's] attentiveness to you."[15] Expressing appreciation and reciprocating attentiveness is key to creating a community of love within our marriages.

Each temperament is different and has its own critical emotional needs; a common error is to assume that your spouse's are the same as yours. When you show appreciation for your spouse, you should focus on the qualities and characteristics that are most inspiring and appealing for that particular temperament, while avoiding the land mines that cause discouragement, hurt feelings, or withdrawal. Understanding your spouse's temperament will give you that focus. Before we look at some temperament combinations, let's take a look at the temperaments individually, as they tend to express themselves in a relationship.

[15] John Paul II, *The Role of the Christian Family in the Modern World*.

The Temperament God Gave You

YOUR CHOLERIC SPOUSE

Petruchio: "*To conclude, we have 'greed so well together,*
That upon Sunday is the wedding day."
Katharina: "*I'll see thee hang'd on Sunday first.*"
(Shakespeare, *The Taming of the Shrew*)

Your choleric spouse is a dynamo, a multi-tasker, a go-getter. He is independent, energetic, forthright, and capable. He is confident, decisive, highly productive, and intelligent. When you first met, he probably had all the great ideas for dates and kept the relationship moving forward. When you married, he probably took charge of the family and business decisions. You might often find yourself wondering (especially if you are a melancholic or a phlegmatic): *Where does he get all that energy?*

A choleric bread-winner may become an entrepreneur — usually starting several businesses. We know a very successful choleric who has eleven kids, owns several businesses, teaches classes at his kids' school, and coaches their sports teams. And he found time to train for the Ironman triathlon! He goes in a hundred directions at once, all with a big smile and a lot of free advice for anyone who might listen. Fortunately, his lovely and highly capable wife manages the home life so that he can be the energetic choleric he is.

The downside is that cholerics can get a little controlling. They can look down on others who are not as naturally productive and energetic. They can lack empathy. They can be overly self-sufficient, and forget to include others in their plans. When you are in a fight with them, you will call them *stubborn*, *prideful*, *opinionated*, *domineering*, and *self-centered*.

Your choleric spouse might have been an aggressive suitor, using all the tricks in the book to win your love. Once married, however, he may become equally aggressive in pursuit of building a future, while you are left wondering what happened to the romance. Your choleric spouse is not against the romantic interlude, but he does need to be reminded of the value of it and to set aside time for it. The choleric is such a one-man (or -woman) show, that it can sometimes be difficult for him to express his genuine need and gratitude for his spouse. Although generally extraverted, he does not like to express his deepest, innermost feelings. This latter aspect of the choleric personality is due, in part, to the fact that cholerics tend to make decisions based on logical principles rather than on feelings, but also because they fear losing control through the vulnerability of expressing deep emotion. Within the supportive and loving environment of the marriage, you can help your choleric spouse learn to explore and express his deepest feelings.

One type of emotion that a choleric may readily express is anger, since it tends to be directed outward. Because impressions leave a deep mark on the choleric and last a long time, anger may last beyond a reasonable time and turn bitter or hateful. In general, anger is an expression of hurt or a reaction to having something of importance trampled upon. A demonstrative choleric may be quick to express anger at others or to make a strong pronouncement of judgment, but reluctant to express emotional pain, which may be the source of the problem. You can encourage your choleric spouse to express his feelings, so that anger and resentment do not build up, exploding in a great outburst of temper. Your nonjudgmental encouragement will help him learn to express his feelings appropriately, to become more trusting, and ultimately to become, in turn, more empathic and understanding of others.

Cholerics often falsely equate meekness with weakness, but meekness is one of the fruits of the Holy Spirit that the choleric will do well to seek. Help your choleric spouse realize that apart from God he can do nothing (John 15:5). To let go of past resentment and anger, the choleric must learn to forgive — as well as to receive forgiveness in the sacrament of Reconciliation. Your choleric spouse will be hard-working and non-complaining in carrying out what he views as his proper share of the duties of marriage. Cholerics have little tolerance for whiners and complainers. In fact, a choleric will take it as a challenge and an insult if his spouse thinks he needs help in an area he views as his "job." In our marriage, for example, Laraine finally forbade Art from doing the laundry — not just because the whites tended to turn pink or blue or some other non-white color, but chiefly because it implied that *she* wasn't doing such a good job and needed some help.

Our friend Martha is a model take-charge mom, a serious professional who balances work and home; she keeps the kids on task, gets everyone to their scheduled appointments and extracurricular activities, maintains ongoing professional training, *and* is a gourmet cook who enjoys entertaining friends. But one day, she noticed that everyone was loafing or watching TV; she was the only one doing the chores. She hit the roof: "That's it! I'm taking a month's sabbatical! You guys are all in charge from now on!" If you tend to rely heavily on a choleric spouse like Martha, beware! Don't let it get to the breaking point before you chip in; and always make sure you express your appreciation for all she does.

Your choleric spouse really hates to ask for help. Sure, he is willing to delegate tasks to expand his sphere of influence and productivity; but asking for help is another story. He views it as admitting a weakness. An understanding spouse will tread gently in these sensitive areas. Be sensitive also to the choleric need for a certain degree of trust before he is willing to reveal deep intimacies about his feelings, insecurities, or weaknesses.

Good spiritual direction, an authentic prayer life (which will help the ever-active choleric learn to "rest in the Lord"), and a "program of life" (a practical, concrete plan for growing in virtue and combating root sins) can help an independent, stubborn choleric to develop some much-needed humility and to discover his interdependence with the other members of the Body of Christ.

∞

*Tips on meeting your choleric
spouse's emotional needs*

• Express appreciation for his achievements and contributions to your family — even if he appears indifferent to such expressions.

• If he gets it right, tell him so.

• Show loyalty. Criticism or sarcasm is viewed as lack of loyalty. Defend your spouse.

• Challenge him to become more empathic and to express appreciation — even when he doesn't agree. Agreement is a judgment about result; empathy is understanding and walking in another's shoes so that he will feel understood.

• Help him to appreciate the processes of relationships (empathy, encouragement, non-judgmental listening) and not just the results.

• Help your choleric spouse find rejuvenating forms of relaxation; he will tend to keep going and going, and even the forms of "relaxation" he chooses can be more of the same.

The Temperament God Gave You

*"You say it's torment to abide her folly
And put up with her pride and melancholy."*
(Chaucer, *Wife of Bath's Prologue*)

Everyone appreciates a melancholic spouse's attention to detail, order, and tidiness — especially when it comes to caring for the home. What tired, world-weary husband doesn't relish coming home to his melancholic wife's perfectly balanced home-cooked dinner in a sparkling, tidy, dust-free home? At 7:30 p.m., the kids are scrubbed — their homework already completed — and tucked in bed. What wife wouldn't appreciate a melancholic husband's attentiveness to a loose floorboard or a squeaky door hinge, his collection of tools organized in the toolbox, ready to fix and repair? The front lawn is a remarkable thick blanket of green, free from crabgrass and thatch, and the kids' toys aren't left out overnight, scattered all over the porch and the driveway, as might be found in a sanguine's home.

Yet perfection demands a price. Your melancholic spouse has to *worry* about making it perfect. With the worry come the pessimistic thoughts and comments. *I saw a red ant today. What if we have an infestation? Megan got an 84 on her last algebra test. I think she is neglecting her studies. I noticed that Mike missed that last shot. He'll never make the team!* While your melancholic spouse sets his standards high, the *disparity* between real life and the ideal often leaves the melancholic disappointed and critical. While the sanguine shrugs off such disparity ("that's life"), and the choleric sees it as a challenge to push harder (and will not take it as a personal failure), the melancholic might either find fault in those around him or be tempted to take it personally and become self-critical or discouraged.

Melancholics value the truth and will often state it quite forthrightly — and then are puzzled when others take offense. Your melancholic spouse may analyze the situation, determine that things are not measuring up exactly as they should, and then make a pronouncement to that effect. Then he wonders why everyone's mood darkens.

The classic melancholic temptation is to put the *affective* aspects of the relationship on the back-burner, for the sake of an ideal. *"But it's the truth!"* is a typical melancholic refrain. (The choleric has a similar temptation, but it is to subjugate the affective to the effective.) Relationship-building, motivation, massaging a situation: these are all slightly foreign to the idealistic, high-minded melancholic.

For example, melancholic Karen's husband came home excitedly one evening, waving Redskins tickets: "My boss gave me two tickets to the game! We haven't gone out together in a year!" "But it's such short notice!" Karen replied. "We can't possibly go this weekend!" Her husband felt very let down and dispirited. From Karen's point of view, she had simply stated the truth. If she had only had more warning. From her husband's perspective, that truth could have been left unsaid, for the sake of their relationship. His enthusiasm for a special date together — even if not optimal — was already waning. Karen found herself discouraged and disappointed that her husband didn't understand how she couldn't just "drop everything" to go out.

Melancholics are motivated by solving problems, but most other people are not. As a result, they may appear to be aloof, judgmental, or overly critical; and they are puzzled when others don't respond to them. A melancholic's nagging or negative comments are usually no more successful at motivating his spouse than a choleric's in-your-face challenges. For example, melancholic

Anna found herself harping for several months on her husband's lack of job initiative. He wasn't living up to his "potential." But all the while she was criticizing, her husband was becoming more and more distant. She was making him feel like a failure and pushing him away from her without realizing what she was doing.

A friend of hers finally helped her to realize that there was an even worthier ideal to pursue than the ideal of "living up to your potential"; namely, the ideal of the "spousal team." Anna's friend told her that she and her husband were a team, and they had to work together to pursue their goals. A team couldn't function with one member taking the entire burden — and the entire blame — on his shoulders. Rather, she needed to do *her part* to help them achieve their financial goals. Anna stopped criticizing and started praising her husband's efforts, and she herself began looking for a part-time job.

You can help your melancholic spouse to see the greater good that will come out of the current situation, problematic though it may seem. In other words, help him see the forest, instead of each twisted and thorny tree. If your melancholic spouse becomes overly critical of you, help him remember that your *relationship* is more important than any situation about which he, in his perfectionism, might be dissatisfied.

Melancholics risk becoming easily disappointed when their spouse does not "live up" to their high expectations. Since the fall of Adam, the melancholic has been doomed to disappointment. Melancholics' temptation is to dwell on the disappointments, becoming extremely self-absorbed, focusing on how things don't measure up to their satisfaction. This can result in a kind of passive-aggressive form of control; when not complaining or criticizing, they are heaving deeply disappointed sighs, rolling their eyes, or suffering in noticeable silence. Or worse: the melancholic wife may be more likely than the other temperaments to punish a spouse for a perceived hurt by withholding intimacy.

Melancholics can also become discouraged by physical ailments. A melancholic may seem to complain more about illness, aches, and pains than people of other temperaments. A choleric spouse will find it quite annoying to hear an ongoing litany of physical complaints and may be even heard to snap, "Stop whining!" or "Get over it!" This sort of reaction will not help the melancholic "snap out of it" — if that were even possible for a melancholic. A sanguine spouse will try to cheer up the melancholic, but even the ebullient sanguine can be worn down as the melancholic ponders and frets over the many possible diseases his current symptoms portend.

This is, in part, due to the fact that melancholics tend to have a lower level of energy, in part because they have a tendency to overanalyze the details, and also because they are more *comfortable* talking about physical ailments than they are about their feelings. Your melancholic spouse may also need more rest than you do (especially if you are an energetic choleric), especially when he's under stress.

Be aware that your melancholic spouse may not always readily reveal *all* that is truly on his mind (especially if he is attempting to subdue some of his overly critical talk). Instead, he may store up the things that are bothering him until he finally has what we call the "melancholic dump." The melancholic dump is when all that is wrong in the world and with your relationship must be disclosed *at this very moment*. Issues build up inside the introverted melancholic until it is no longer possible to remain silent. It can be painful for all parties.

Help your melancholic spouse avoid global despair by responding empathically, showing that you want to understand his perspective, and by developing a lighthearted manner and a sense of humor about the foibles of life. Take Matthew 6:34 as your motto: "Do not worry about tomorrow; tomorrow will take care of itself. Sufficient for a day is its own evil." Remind your melancholic spouse that it is not likely that everything horrible that can happen will happen all at once. Help him see the silver lining in the dark cloud. By checking with your spouse regularly and asking him what is on his mind or what is bothering him, he will feel more understood, and you will be more likely to avoid the build-up that precedes the dreaded melancholic dump.

You can help your melancholic spouse come out of his despairing moments by developing and sharing your own sense of humor, by showing him the bigger (relationship) picture, and by empathically responding to his concerns, instead of trying to argue him out of those concerns — or even worse, by belittling them. Your melancholic spouse might not ask for appreciation, but he will flower when he receives it. It's not always easy to show appreciation to melancholics. They tend to be highly critical themselves, and they do not respond with big smiles and hugs when they are complimented. They might even stoically *dismiss* your compliments — out of fear of acknowledging their deep feelings, or because they don't believe they deserve praise, or because they don't wish to succumb to the sin of pride. Or it might be because they give so little praise themselves. All of these factors combine to leave the melancholic's "love tank" very low on words of appreciation, which, in turn, gives rise to stoicism, criticism, and an even greater sense of discouragement. It is absolutely imperative to break through this downward cycle. And although it is a simple prescription, it can be very difficult in practice to shower an introverted, critical melancholic with words of affirmation and appreciation.

Understanding Your Spouse's Temperament

∞

First things first

Although someone of any of the four temperaments might say that "first things must come first," this is especially true for the melancholic. If the melancholic neglects the most important things, he will become grumpy, critical, discouraged, and possibly even depressed. But procrastinating on important issues will only make a melancholic suffer greater frustration. You can help him set aside time to work on the important issues; sometimes he might need your help getting started.

And one of *the* most important things is the melancholic's faith. A melancholic may be tempted to see faith as a series of dictums and prescriptions. But Christianity is not first about dogma or a set of rules, but about a person. Jesus Christ is the way, the truth, and the life. It is vitally important for the analytical, detailed, and perfectionist melancholic to develop a personal relationship with Christ. Otherwise, he might end up becoming judgmental, self-critical, and scrupulous. For example, an adult child of a melancholic shared with us the sad tale of how several of her siblings left the practice of the Catholic Faith: when they were younger, their father had forced all his children to practice a rigorous (and unreasonable, given their young age) set of devotions under threat of punishment if they did not perform them with perfection.

As the spouse of a melancholic, you should understand that his tendency to dwell on the negative doesn't mean that he is completely unhappy, and it doesn't mean that he doesn't appreciate you. By showing your appreciation for him, you will become a model for the introverted melancholic. By showing him empathy (even when it is not at first reciprocated), you will show him that you care enough to want to really understand his perspective. Simply insisting, "It's not as bad as you think" or "Lighten up!" will not achieve the desired effect, because it does not prove that you have *understood* the way the melancholic sees the situation. Empathic listening — which means that you first indicate that you have understood what your spouse is saying (by repeating back to him in your own words what you hear him saying) — is one way to show your understanding. This will enable your spouse to move beyond the criticism and complaints toward accepting a possible solution to the situation. Eventually, your empathy, your appreciation, and your positive example will help him begin to see situations and people in a more positive light.

∞

*Tips on meeting your melancholic
spouse's emotional needs*

• Affirm him — even when he doesn't ask for it.

• Provide opportunities for solitude, reflection, and rejuvenation (through acts of service).

• Offer support and appreciation: tell him you know he has a lot to contribute and he can achieve his goals, even though he might feel discouraged or apprehensive.

• Strive for order and fairness: your melancholic spouse needs order (and will usually create it for himself) and can be upset by instances of unfairness or injustice (which are, in a sense, disorder on a larger, societal scale).

• Be radically accepting of him as a *person,* and not just of his ideas and views.

Understanding Your Spouse's Temperament

YOUR SANGUINE SPOUSE

"There's little of the melancholy element in her,
my lord: she is never sad but when she sleeps; and
not ever sad then; for I have heard my daughter
say, she hath often dreamed of unhappiness,
and waked herself with laughing."

(Shakespeare, *Much Ado About Nothing*)

Your sanguine spouse probably made the courtship a whirlwind of romance and excitement. If you aren't also a sanguine, you were probably attracted to the novelty of so much "fun." Your sanguine spouse draws out your interpersonal, fun-loving side. He will make sure you have plenty of friends (and often invite them over for dinner), will plan romantic evenings for just the two of you, and will see to it that you don't skip a vacation.

When you are down in the dumps, he will lift your spirits. He is committed to open communication, dialogue, and creative problem-solving. A sanguine spouse will welcome children into the world with joy and loving attention, and will allow them all the freedom they need to develop happily with lots of encouragement and action. Other kids will say to yours, "Gee, I wish my mom [or dad] were as much fun as yours! Mine is so uncool!" A sanguine parent values what most kids value: friendship and fun. The kids will have play dates and co-ops, rewards for good behavior, extracurricular activities galore, and lots of open communication. Your kids will truly thrive.

On the other hand, you might have to keep tabs on the checkbook for your sanguine spouse. Sanguines are not known for their budgeting skills, and financial strain can definitely put a crimp in their style. And don't move out to the country. Where are the *neighbors?* Sanguine parents sometimes find themselves accused of taking the kids' side; when told of classroom antics, they are as likely to laugh as they are to punish the offender.

∞

Try to keep the sanguine focused

Sanguines also imagine that they can fit more activities into their schedules than is actually feasible, within the laws of physics. If the phone rings just as they are walking out the door, they will answer it — and still believe they can get to their appointment on time. As a result, sanguines tend to rush into meetings late, carrying their Starbucks, apologizing profusely, and laughing about some little incident that occurred while they were zipping through traffic. Sanguines have a seemingly inborn ability for reframing unfortunate mishaps in a humorous light, turning their own foibles into comic moments, and diffusing anger directed against themselves.

It can be quite annoying when a sanguine spouse gets that urge to accomplish something stupendous within an impossibly short time frame — and then the spouse gets dragged in to clean up the mess. For example, our son was having his sixteenth birthday party, and it was going to be a big affair. The house was decorated, the food had been purchased, and the entire tenth-grade class was due to arrive in two hours. Sanguine Laraine decided that the party would not be complete without a ping-pong table. Melancholic Art was sent out grumbling to find a ping-pong table, purchase it, bring it home, and put it together — all before the kids arrived! Like many sanguine ventures, the project was much larger than anticipated. When the first kids arrived, Art was still putting together the table. Thankfully, one of the parents volunteered his expertise, and the table was finally assembled — not without many dire pronouncements from beleaguered Art.

Adult sanguines sometimes wonder whether their impulsivity and distractibility is really an undiagnosed case of attention deficit disorder. One sanguine we know tells a funny story about an accident (fortunately, not serious) that occurred while he was speeding down the interstate (late, again!), talking on his cell phone (to another sanguine), while smoking a cigar. It was a classic sanguine moment, but one that probably led to some anxious moments for his wife!

When you are angry or having a disagreement, you might accuse your sanguine spouse of being flighty, scatterbrained, immature, superficial, "all talk and no follow-through," and spending *way* too much time on the phone. Is she interested in nothing more than shopping? Can't he stick to *one* project until it has been completed?

"Whenever Joyce runs into a neighbor, she is likely to invite them over for dinner that evening!" complained melancholic Steve about his sanguine wife. "I just want to spend a quiet evening at home!" Steve wanted to know just how many parties he was going to have to attend during the Christmas season for Joyce to be happy.

"How many are truly *necessary?*" Art asked Joyce.

"Two," was the answer.

"Can you handle two, Steve — *without* complaining?" Art continued.

"Sure," Steve replied. "If I was expecting five parties, two would be a piece of cake!" We had to work out a deal that it would be fine for Joyce to attend the additional three parties alone. But if it meant going to two with a happy Steve, it was worth it for Joyce.

Joyce wanted Steve to stop being such a grump every time they went on vacation. "I have too much to worry about," said Steve. "But you ruin every vacation," complained Joyce. For a melancholic to let slide all vital matters for a week or two was simply asking too much. So, we worked out a compromise whereby Steve would accomplish three vitally important things early in the morning each day of his vacation, so he could relax and be happy the rest of the day.

The sanguine/melancholic couple is a classic case of "opposites attracting." The choleric/phlegmatic is another example. We tend not to fall in love with people who are just like ourselves. Complementarity can lead to attraction, even if it also requires greater effort at mutual understanding.

During their romantic phase, each saw in the other something vital: the sanguine provided joy, and the melancholic gave the sanguine much-need depth. Yet over time, if the couple doesn't keep in mind the beauty they originally found in the other or cultivate an appreciation for each other's unique gifts, as the bloom of romance begins to fade, they become irritated about the very things that originally attracted them. *She is too superficial and only wants to have fun; she doesn't understand that there are problems in this world; she never wants to look at some of the tough situations we face. She doesn't understand how much a burden this job is for me.*

The sanguine, for his part, may complain that he is tired of being the one who *always* has to do the uplifting in the relationship; his spouse *never* wants simply to have fun, *never* has anything positive to say, and *always* dwells on the negative.

Take care that these "absolutes" do not become entrenched in your way of thinking about and responding to each other, for they cause defensiveness and prohibit empathy. Instead, remind yourself how much less fulfilled your life would be without the joy and vivacity of his temperament. Focus on the many ways your sanguine spouse adds wonder, spontaneity, and adventure to your marriage.

Attentiveness to interpersonal relationships, a natural priority for the sanguine, enhances the *communion of persons* that a marriage is called to become. As John Paul II writes, "interpersonal relationship[s] . . . bring into play not only a person's capacity to know, but also the deeper capacity to entrust oneself to others, to enter into a relationship with them that is intimate and enduring."[16]

∞

*Tips on meeting your sanguine
spouse's emotional needs*

• Make joy a priority and not a frivolity. Enjoy fun times with your spouse (don't always be a wet blanket — especially you melancholics!).

• Give plenty of overt attention and displays of affection.

• Tell him you appreciate his optimism and enthusiasm.

• Go on a weekly date with your sanguine spouse to connect on an intimate, even romantic level, and to deepen the emotional intimacy between the two of you.

• Allow your spouse to entertain friends or volunteer for church or community, but help him not become "over-extended."

• Support your sanguine spouse when the details become overwhelming or when he needs to undertake a long-term, in-depth project.

[16] John Paul II, *Fides et Ratio*, 332.

YOUR PHLEGMATIC SPOUSE
"I know you have a gentle, noble temper,
A soul as even as a calm."
(Shakespeare, *King Henry VIII*)

"What a great guy!" is the common refrain about a phlegmatic. When you were dating, he was an attentive admirer, always concerned about your feelings. He was your rock, the calm, steady fellow with the respectful manner and solid character. Your parents were pleased, for they suspected he would make a devoted husband and father. He was always willing to go along with all of your ideas for activities and events, and you appreciated his easy-going cooperation. Now that you are married, you find that he takes his share of domestic chores, is calm when the toddler needs a midnight trip to the emergency room, and rarely initiates a quarrel.

Your phlegmatic spouse is faithful, takes commitment seriously, places a high priority on peace and harmony in the home, and rarely complains. He will put aside his own needs or desires to be at the service of his spouse. He is dedicated, loyal, and a good parent.

As the years go by, however, you may begin to find him a bit distant. He doesn't want to talk after work but goes straight to the television or his computer, and too often leaves you to solve domestic problems by yourself. You sense a certain indifference or passivity and a lack of intimacy. To get him to be more active, you begin to nag, demand, or complain. It seems that he is beginning to avoid you. Sometimes it takes a major "melt-down" just to get a response. He always says he will take care of what you ask, but you sense that he is stubbornly retreating into his own shell. When you ask what is going on, he says, "I don't know," or "Nothing." He seems distant and apathetic. You begin to wonder, "Does he even care about me?"

When the phlegmatic wife has babies and toddlers, the temptation is to let her appearance — and the appearance of the home — go. She might find herself too overwhelmed to attend to these details. This is a dangerous trap to fall into, especially if she has married a critical, detail-oriented melancholic! His criticism will engender more silent stubbornness, and a sense of futility or failure. The vicious cycle of criticism and withdrawal can result in a messy home, with both spouses bitter and angry.

Francine is a melancholic who appreciated phlegmatic Larry's congenial nature, his patience, and his steady, predictable demeanor. In the early years of their marriage, he helped out with the kids, never complained about working hard, and was happy to cater to Francine's needs and the needs of the children. He was thoughtful, loyal, and unobtrusive. As the children grew and the family's needs expanded, Francine became concerned that Larry wasn't ambitious enough at work or at home. His promotions and raises did not keep up with their growing expenses; he seemed more withdrawn at home, less enthusiastic, and less communicative.

Since both Francine and Larry were introverts, they were tempted to let these problems simmer, hoping they would work themselves out. But the couple grew less intimate and became more and more distant. Francine started to complain about her unhappiness and his lack of initiative. But this didn't motivate Larry; rather, it discouraged him. When he became discouraged, he grew more distant and less open. She responded with criticism, and he withdrew even more; the cycle continued.

Problems with a phlegmatic spouse often center on issues of intimacy and motivation. How to encourage disclosure and initiative in someone so preoccupied with stability and peace? The temptation to nag or exert pressure is a poor long-term strategy, one that will only further send the phlegmatic into his shell.

The Temperament God Gave You

What works, then? *Radical appreciation and confidence-boosting.* Tell him what you like before you tell him where he falls short. Build him up with generous words of praise. The phlegmatic, *more than any of the other temperaments*, feels hurt when a loved one criticizes him. After all, he is always trying to please. He is always the nice guy. Our son helped us understand this when we came down particularly hard on him once, for planning a date without consulting us. He felt that he was always so responsible, so cooperative and willing to abide by the rules; how could we be so critical of him? If we had only been more explicit at the outset, he told us, about *our* expectations and guidelines, he would have been happy to meet them.

In *Why Marriages Succeed or Fail,* John Gottman describes three styles of marriage that work: the conflict avoider, the volatile, and the validating. Interestingly, he argues that whichever of these styles the marriage takes, the key to success is that for every one negative comment or interaction, there should be *five* positive ones. Marriages need a lot of appreciation and encouragement and a lot of positive communication *about good things.* Phlegmatics as well as melancholics need to stretch themselves to be overtly appreciative.

As we mentioned in the section on the melancholic spouse, introverted temperaments (melancholic and phlegmatic) can have the most difficulty in expressing appreciation of their spouse, and in expressing their need to receive confidence-boosting words of affirmation. If left to their own devices, they can fall into a pattern of criticism (melancholic) or silence (phlegmatic). In an effort to engage an impassive phlegmatic, the frustrated spouse begins to nag, complain, or demand — which results in the dreaded cycle of nagging and withdrawal. How to break the nagging cycle? Positive communication!

Understanding Your Spouse's Temperament

∞

End the nagging cycle!

Break out of the nagging cycle through confidence-building. Phlegmatics do not respond to threats of disaster or arduous challenges. Where a choleric might respond in kind, or a melancholic dig in, the phlegmatic will withdraw. If you build up your phlegmatic spouse's confidence with many words of encouragement and affirmation, he will feel ready to take on a difficult task or answer what hitherto seemed like an impossible request. Before making any criticism or giving out a demanding assignment, you should always first build up his confidence by reminding him of the ways in which he resolved such difficulties in the past, or how much you depend on and appreciate his hard work and support.

Secondly, you need to be specific. "I really appreciate all that work you did on the lawn last year. I really think our lawn is looking a lot better now. I would really appreciate if you could get rid of this spot of clover that seems to be spreading." Or "I really appreciate how nice you have been with my mom. I know that is really hard for you. But we really need to get this house cleaned up for her visit." A vague or general goal is too nebulous and uncertain for the cautious phlegmatic. "Why can't you be more communicative?" or "Why aren't you taking the initiative with our kids?" is unhelpful and unmotivating. Give your phlegmatic a specific target, and build him up with the confidence to achieve it. Sometimes, partnering helps a phlegmatic get moving. "How about if I take the first whack at updating your resume, and then you can take it from there?" Or: "Let's go together for a jog!" Build momentum based on words of affirmation and loving appreciation instead of the unsuccessful model of trying to motivate by criticism.

If your spouse is phlegmatic, it is very likely that he will prefer the "conflict avoider" style of marriage. Now, if you yourself have a volatile nature or are very assertive when it comes to expressing your views and wishes, you may find yourself facing defensiveness and withdrawal. Remember the five-to-one ratio, and make sure you show your spouse plenty of interest, affection, appreciation, concern, empathy, and acceptance, as well as making small acts of kindness and lighthearted playfulness. Help him to express his innermost feelings in a context of respect and affection.

Your phlegmatic spouse is dependable and cooperative. But he needs your help in developing his own interests and enthusiasms through positive motivation, respect, and support.

Encourage your phlegmatic spouse to get sufficient exercise and to eat well. Keeping fit is often more of a challenge for the placid, slow-moving phlegmatic than for the other temperaments.

∞

Praise and affirmation move mountains

This is one temperament that really needs to be pumped up and shown a lot of appreciation. Your phlegmatic spouse will thrive with good, old-fashioned, sweet-talking praise. Commit to inspiring your phlegmatic spouse: movies, tapes, ideas that move the spirit. The phlegmatic needs to be *internally motivated;* that is, he needs to love the goal and be convinced that he is the one who can do it. Other temperaments can be motivated by externals: the choleric will respond to a challenge, the melancholic by a deadline, for example. But the phlegmatic can become an unmovable object — despite external pressure (which often exacerbates the phlegmatic resistance). When a wife has been nagging her phlegmatic husband for weeks to get started on the taxes (certainly not inspiring, nor is it something he would *love* to do), he winds up simply ignoring her. But when he feels appreciated, needed, and confident, he will begin to work on the taxes *out of love for her.*

Phlegmatics benefit the most from supportive and uplifting structures. Team sports, private schools, the military, religious organizations, corporations, and other structured environments with clear-cut goals and built-in rewards benefit the phlegmatic. The same is true in the spiritual realm. Phlegmatics find that they can grow spiritually with structure, goals, and personal attention. Organizations such as the Knights of Columbus, which provide specific activities and ways to help the Church apostolically, are well suited to this temperament. When a phlegmatic is asked personally to help out in a parish activity, this is also very motivating. The phlegmatic often finds that the structure of a Church organization (provided it is not a distant, impersonal one) will give him the avenue he needs to find his specific place within the parish or the Church as a whole; and this will allow him the necessary motivation to work actively in the apostolate and to grow more deeply in his personal relationship with Christ.

∞

*Tips on meeting your phlegmatic
spouse's emotional needs*

• Acknowledge him openly, especially his easy-going nature and his sensitivity to others' needs; use *words of affirmation*.

• Give him time for relaxation.

• Praise him when he takes a leadership stance; *boost his confidence* to continue taking on challenges.

• Use gentle reminders, but don't nag him, dump on him, criticize him, or take over for him.

• Be *specific* in your requests, and state them *positively*.

Chapter 5

∞

Temperament Combinations in Marriage

"The Lord God said: 'It is not good
for the man to be alone. I will
make a suitable partner for him.' "
Genesis 2:18

"Two are better than one. . . . If the one falls,
the other will lift up his companion."
Ecclesiastes 4:9

"Behind every successful man is a woman.
Behind her is his wife."
Groucho Marx

∞

What happens when a melancholic marries a sanguine? Or a choleric marries a phlegmatic? Is it true that "opposites attract"?

The most diametrically opposed temperament pairings are the melancholic/sanguine and the phlegmatic/choleric. They are completely opposite in all key areas: intensity, quickness of response, and duration of response to internal or external stimuli.

Sometimes temperament differences can give rise to serious misunderstandings in the early stages of a relationship. For example, a melancholic friend shared with us the following situation, which illustrates a classic melancholic/sanguine clash: A sanguine man she was dating had promised to call her while he was on a business trip. However, when he called, it was from a bar, and she could barely hear him over the noise. It was his only chance to call, and he wanted to keep his promise, but she was horrified. "How could he?!" she exclaimed. "He called from a bar!" I reminded her that he *did* call; surely that was a sign that he missed her. "How much can he be missing me, if he is calling from a bar?" was all she could say.

Temperament differences are not *in themselves* enough to make or break a relationship. We can readily imagine how two people of opposite temperaments might find each other attractive in the initial phases of the relationship. They each see in the other a critical characteristic that is lacking in their own temperament. The quiet, peaceful, unassuming phlegmatic is attracted to the dynamic, opinionated, problem-solving choleric. The organized, introspective, and analytical melancholic discovers the exciting, fun-loving, outgoing sanguine. But, what happens when they each discover the opposite temperament's weaknesses? What happens when the peaceful phlegmatic has to live with the argumentative choleric? What happens when the fun-loving sanguine has to cheer up her beloved melancholic every day? Can this hold up over time?

Many people marry someone of the opposite temperament, and do manage to build happy, long-lasting marital relationships. That's because what is most important is that your spouse's *values* and *beliefs* — not his temperament — are the same as yours. Yet complementarity in temperament is generally a boon to relationships, provided the partners develop mutual respect for their different styles. A family is enriched by having varied approaches and perspectives on a situation.

For example, when some tough-minded troubleshooting is needed, let's ask the melancholic for some advice. If a situation needs lightening up and some fun, enter the sanguine. Indeed, having a spouse of the opposite temperament can enrich your marriage in varied ways, providing both delights and challenges to grow.

∞

Opposites can attract . . . and annoy

Each temperament can provide something of great value, but some situations will favor one temperament over another. In a climate of mutual respect and overt expressions of appreciation, there will be less defensiveness and less imposition of power or control by one temperament over the other. When two become one in the sacrament of marriage, complementary temperaments will add depth of perception and varied responses to any given situation.

For example: initially, the melancholic sees in the sanguine an opportunity for much-needed joy. He appreciates the enthusiasm, the lightheartedness, and the optimism. The melancholic, who has a tendency to despair, will find the sanguine's optimism uplifting. The sanguine in turn will appreciate the depth and interior life of the melancholic. He brings depth to the relationship and offers unheard-of insights into human nature (which naturally appeals to the interpersonal sanguine) and glimpses into theology and philosophy — levels of thought rarely approached by the typically scattered sanguine.

As the years go by, children are born, and work becomes more challenging and stressful. Small issues that were previously overlooked may turn into obstacles to intimacy. These challenges either help the couple learn how to grow in their communication, or else they become sources of conflict. The sanguine is now considered superficial and scattered, and the melancholic becomes negative and depressing. The key is to learn new ways of communicating, showing appreciation, and motivating, so that the couple can grow ever closer, rather than apart.

Patti, a lively but disorganized sanguine-phlegmatic, married Charles, an intelligent and decisive choleric-melancholic, after a whirlwind courtship. He was unlike anyone in her entire family; in fact, she had never met anyone so disciplined, organized, thoughtful, and principled as he. Her youthful college days had been breezy, fun-loving, and haphazard. He provided everything she lacked. After they had their first child, however, she became more and more aware of the fact that her temperament was not naturally suited to the demands of her new married life. Running a household required discipline, order, and organization. No more staying up all night talking with friends, no more hours spent socializing or shopping — and no more fun! Charles began to criticize her lack of homemaking ability: Can't she keep up the checkbook? Why are the morning dishes still in the sink when he comes home from work? Why did he never have any clean clothes to wear? What was she *doing* all day?

Patti blamed her family of origin: why had she never been taught how to run a household? She would start out doing the dishes, get distracted by a phone call, and then haphazardly throw a load of laundry into the washer. She was feeling exhausted, because she had gotten up early with Charles to fix him breakfast. By noon, she was ready for a nap . . . and nothing had been done. She was frustrated and unfulfilled, and so was Charles, who came home to a messy house and no dinner on the table.

Patti needed to develop confidence in her temperament's greatest qualities: relationship-building, communication, and joy. She needed to take one small step at a time to achieve skills in the organizational sphere. Instead of keeping the entire house spotless and dust-free, with a gourmet dinner planned every night, Charles needed only to have one main room tidy and a decent meal on the table. Charles could appreciate how calm and nurturing Patti was with the baby, and realized that perfect order was secondary to a loving, peaceful home. They both realized they needed some fun, romantic "couple time," so they built in a monthly date night, away from the pressures of home and work, to reconnect in the romantic and loving way they had when they were first dating.

This story represents a common experience for "polar opposite" couples. At first, each spouse enjoys the qualities of the other's temperament. But over time and in the face of challenges, these same qualities are viewed in a negative light: *She always wants to have her way; I can never do what I want. She is pushy and driven; can't we have a quiet evening at home? She seems to thrive on conflict; I just want peace and quiet and everyone to be happy. He, on the other hand, is so passive, so unassertive. Why can't he take charge of the situation? Why do I always have to solve the problems and handle the hard stuff? He is just lazy and unmotivated.* Understanding the unique characteristics and demands of temperament combinations can help couples appreciate their differences and avoid falling into communication ruts that only provoke and prolong the unhealthy stereotypical responses.

Melancholic John and sanguine Mary have learned to appreciate the peculiarities of each other's temperaments — even to laugh about them. One Saturday afternoon, Mary and I were leaving a half-day silent retreat (a great effort for two sanguines!) and were headed for the parking lot. I was impressed when Mary jumped into a bright red Miata convertible — an appropriate car for a sanguine! "But it's not my car," said Mary. "It's my melancholic husband's." John allows his sanguine wife to drive his convertible, provided she abides by his stringent melancholic's rules, which fall just short of requiring orange plastic cones to be placed around the parking spot. Mary says, "It may be a car for a sanguine, but his rules limit the amount of fun any true, carefree sanguine could have in it" (although Mary admits that these rules have kept the car in optimum condition for thirteen years).

∞

Spousal temperaments overview
Before we examine the spousal temperament combinations in depth, let's take a quick look at some of the common traits of spouses of each temperament.

CHOLERIC SPOUSE

• **Overview:** Extraverted. Productive; zealous; pragmatic; intense; confrontational. Loyalty and acknowledgment of achievements are critical.

• **Strengths:** Natural leader, motivator, and initiator. Quick learner and adept at many things. Ambitious; driven to succeed.

• **Weaknesses:** Can be overbearing, prideful, controlling, and dismissive. Resists situations of vulnerability. Needs encouragement to express deepest feelings. Needs help in softening his blunt, sometimes harsh, tongue.

• **Hints:** Marriage retreats or enrichment can help this dynamic individual to slow down and focus on the important relationships. Spiritual direction will keep the choleric from becoming single-minded in the wrong direction.

SANGUINE SPOUSE

• **Overview:** Extraverted. Optimistic; interested; creative; adventurous; fun-loving. Seeks joy and happiness in relationships.

• **Strengths:** Outgoing; involved; enthusiastic; eager to please. Heavy priority on relationships; can become actively involved in hosting, entertaining, volunteering, and networking. Values others' feelings. Great with kids.

• **Weaknesses:** Can be superficial, scattered, lacking follow-through. Will prefer fun over duty. Outside activities can make the sanguine neglect home duties.

• **Hints:** Needs attention and affection. Needs encouragement to seek reflection, depth of knowledge, and follow-through. Out of love for Christ, the sanguine will be self-sacrificing, generous, and committed to building a nurturing, loving home.

MELANCHOLIC SPOUSE

+ **Overview:** Introverted. Loves truth, justice, principles. Reflective; slow to react or initiate. Wants the right thing done the right way. Not a follower or a joiner.

+ **Strengths:** Strives for an orderly, organized home life. Loyal to family. Sees marriage as a high calling and a serious responsibility.

+ **Weaknesses:** Willing to complain but hesitant to change. Can overkill on the small stuff and be demanding instead of motivating. Can get discouraged, even depressed over people and situations not living up to the ideal. Tendency to perfectionism — which sometimes includes trying to "perfect" other people.

+ **Hints:** Needs encouragement in seeing the critical importance of relationship-building over doing things the "right way." Strong personal relationship with Christ and a deep prayer life will help the melancholic be more joyful and less critical and demanding of spouse and children.

PHLEGMATIC SPOUSE

+ **Overview:** Introverted. Loves harmony, peace, cooperation. Calm; even-tempered; respectful.

+ **Strengths:** True blue. Supportive in an indirect and quiet way. Dutiful and dedicated. Always seeks peace in relationships.

+ **Weaknesses:** Tendency to take the blame, rather than confront. Can minimize or overlook problems. Can be hesitant to take charge and gets discouraged easily. Sometimes appears distant or indifferent. Tendency to laziness.

• **Hints:** Needs much encouragement to take on leadership and disciplinary roles in the family, and also needs lots of praise and appreciation. Must not be nagged; this will discourage, not motivate.

∞

Now, what happens when two more similar temperaments marry; for example, a melancholic and a phlegmatic? What about marriages in which each spouse is exactly the same temperament? Let's look at some of these combinations.

CHOLERIC/CHOLERIC

The two of you are dynamos, good communicators (although not necessarily in an intimate or supportive fashion), and highly productive. You are both independent, and not emotionally needy. Take care to spend time with each other, in building your relationship, not just "doing."

Learn to listen, instead of having the last word. Try not to engage in useless debates or arguments in which neither of you will back down. Allow yourselves different areas in which to compete and control, so that you are not stepping on each other's toes. Learn the art of forgiveness, and do not dwell on injuries and hurts. Affirm each other's contributions to the family and to society.

You both want to be successful and to achieve great things. Acknowledge the other spouse when he is right. Take time to slow down, smell the roses, and have an evening of catching up, or you may wind up operating on parallel tracks without ever touching base. Learn to explore each other's deepest feelings and desires. Learn to let go of past transgressions. Make a marriage renewal retreat once a year.

SANGUINE/CHOLERIC

The two of you will have a great opportunity to balance fun with productivity and follow-through — if you work together. You are good communicators, optimistic about life, and open to adventure. The fun-loving spouse will help the driven spouse to learn to relax and have fun. Since the choleric is often intense, the sanguine can help him learn to be more sensitive to others and to enjoy himself.

Both will be up for adventure and change, and lots of on-the-go activity. Make sure you allow time just to be together (even though not "productively" in the choleric's opinion).

Both have to work hard at listening and at developing interpersonal depth: the choleric because he fears self-disclosure and the sanguine through lack of introspection — resulting in too much "doing" and not enough "being" for this couple. The choleric may be tempted to exert control over the flightier sanguine (who will resist control) or to criticize, or may simply forget to be appreciative. Criticism wounds sanguines deeply, although they are also very forgiving. Cholerics do not like criticism either, but will hold on to hurt feelings.

The choleric can help the sanguine stay on task, become more focused, develop intellectual depth, and be more discerning. Allow the sanguine spouse opportunities to be the center of attention and give lots of appreciation. The sanguine can help the choleric "lighten up," learn to be more intimate in relationships and to value friendship, and to be more flexible, spontaneous, positive, and accepting of others.

MELANCHOLIC/CHOLERIC

You will both have strong commitment to your relationship. You will relate well on the level of ideals and ideas. But your approaches to work and your motivational styles are very different. The choleric is the action-oriented spouse, while the melancholic takes a long time to change and move. Sometimes, the melancholic's slowness and lack of responsiveness will frustrate the choleric.

The choleric's pragmatism and outcome-orientation may offend the melancholic's love of truth and justice. The choleric will be willing to bend rules, in the interest of achieving a greater good, whereas the melancholic will not. The melancholic will value security, while the choleric may be intrigued by adventure; yet both are responsible. Both spouses will hold on to hurts for a long time, so learn to forgive and forget. The choleric can be blunt, while the melancholic takes a long time to say what he means, and is easily wounded. Cholerics might react angrily to melancholics' pessimistic complaints, sensing a lack of loyalty or criticism.

Both are leaders, and mutual appreciation of this fact is critical. The choleric may try to take the lead in this relationship, with the melancholic exerting subtle, even passive-aggressive, control. The melancholic should try not to withdraw, or be overly critical or piously rigid, or the choleric may become oppositional. The choleric spouse needs to understand that nobody is as productive as he is. Melancholics have a hard time expressing appreciation, but cholerics really need a lot of appreciation. Melancholics need help with decision-making, and with initiating change. Cholerics must learn to take the time to listen.

PHLEGMATIC/CHOLERIC

This is a classic case of "opposites attracting" and is a common combination. The choleric is drawn to the peaceful, calm, and good-natured phlegmatic, while the phlegmatic is drawn to the choleric's energy and take-charge temperament. The phlegmatic will be the relationship-oriented spouse (although not overtly) while the choleric will focus more on "doing." At first, the phlegmatic will learn to enjoy many new activities introduced by the choleric, but later he can become resentful if no time is left for his own initiatives. Beware of overloading the phlegmatic with too many social or stressful activities, which the choleric may thrive on, as they will tire the phlegmatic out.

The choleric probably enjoyed the feeling of running the show when first dating; but after a while, the phlegmatic's natural tendency to passivity can begin to annoy the choleric spouse. If the choleric is a woman and the phlegmatic a man, the untypical gender roles may later have the choleric pushing and criticizing (even contemptuously) to get the phlegmatic to "step up" and be more assertive. The phlegmatic should try not to let it annoy him when the choleric argues or controls, but should help the choleric partner learn to relax. Overcome the temptation to let the choleric do whatever he wants. The phlegmatic should learn to take charge overtly and not use passive-aggressive tactics to get what he wants.

Be aware that the phlegmatic, while willing to follow the choleric's lead, must develop his own interests. Encourage the phlegmatic by positive motivation and respect. One danger is that neither spouse will become intimate on the level of deepest feelings; take time out to explore feelings in secure environment, uncritically. Sit down at a peaceful, romantic dinner and examine each other's goals, desires, deepest feelings within the context of loving support.

SANGUINE/SANGUINE
Laissez les bon temps rouler! You will have a lot of fun together! You will enjoy activities, friends, spontaneous parties and romantic

getaways. Sanguines love to invite others to join in their fun as well: games, beach houses, ski resorts. They value freedom, adventure, and excitement.

It is more common, however, for the sanguine/sanguine relationship to be one of friendship, rather than the serious commitment of marriage. When two sanguines marry, someone will have to run the house and keep a budget. Too many spontaneous surprises, trips, and purchases will cut into any savings. Because sanguines like to be surrounded by friends and action, intimacy may be more difficult to come by. This can result in a hectic, wild, haphazard lifestyle, with no one minding the kids or the home. Too much flexibility and not enough planning and organization can result in a chaotic family life.

Make time for good spiritual and intellectual formation for both of you. Don't get too caught up in worldly or superficial activities, because a marriage can't be based only on the "good times." When the tough times come, be prepared with strong spiritual and familial support. Watch that checkbook!

MELANCHOLIC/SANGUINE

You each have something foreign — but very attractive — to the other: the sanguine's optimism and sense of adventure appeals to the more moody, plodding melancholic. In turn, the melancholic offers depth and introspection, principles and follow-through to the flightier sanguine. The sanguine will help the melancholic to be more optimistic and experience joy in life, and the melancholic will help the sanguine achieve high ideals and a much-needed depth of soul.

Know that your sanguine spouse is not a perfectionist and is not driven by ideals, but is eager for relationships and fun. Sanguines want you to enjoy what they enjoy and to have fun being with them. Communication is vital for the sanguine, so don't withdraw. Melancholics can retreat into their own thoughts and leave the talkative sanguine frustrated. Too much criticism will turn the naturally happy sanguine into a fretting, indecisive, self-doubter. The sanguine needs to realize that the melancholic is introverted, deeply thoughtful, and needs a lot of personal space. Don't push him into parties, friendships, and activities that you enjoy. Learn to compromise. Give the melancholic spouse lots of space and time in which to communicate his inmost thoughts. Allow for his creative silences.

The sanguine tends to tease, while the melancholic's feelings are easily hurt. Don't make fun of the melancholic or expect him to laugh at all your jokes. Don't take his moods personally, especially the tendency to dwell on problems. The sanguine can help to cheer up the melancholic with a lighthearted approach and a sense of humor. Sometimes, the sanguine feels stuck in a role of always having to be the cheerleader; what if the sanguine needs cheering up? If you're the melancholic, try not to be a cross for your sanguine spouse. The sanguine can help the melancholic rise above the day-to-day trials and see joy in the relationship and in life.

PHLEGMATIC/SANGUINE

You both love harmony and peacefulness, and place a high degree of value on good feelings within the relationship. The phlegmatic will be introverted about expressing these feelings, while the sanguine will want to talk. But neither will be too demanding on the other. The danger is that you will skim the surface — the sanguine because it is easier to be superficial and you are easily distracted, and phlegmatic because you don't want to stir up conflict or unpleasant feelings. There may be a significant lack of motivation to achieve great or noble goals.

Both will enjoy friendships, but the phlegmatic will not want to invest too much emotional energy. Give the phlegmatic space and time in which to have peace and quiet. Help the phlegmatic enjoy your activities and friends; he is very cooperative. Over time, the sanguine may accuse the phlegmatic of being boring, and the phlegmatic may feel the sanguine is overwrought and drawn to too many new experiences. The phlegmatic spouse needs to extend himself and do special things with the sanguine spouse. Special occasions are vital: anniversaries, romantic evenings out, birthdays. The phlegmatic should try not to give into grumpy moods or the need to veg out after work.

The sanguine should be aware that the phlegmatic's quietness or lack of expression does not imply lack of appreciation and love. The phlegmatic may require coaxing, but try not to nag. In turn, the phlegmatic needs to develop ways of communicating and better expressing his feelings. Of the two, the sanguine may be the less committed to the relationship, while the phlegmatic is very dedicated and responsible and takes commitment and the sacrament seriously. Both of you may need to work on deepening the spiritual life, but will go about it differently. The sanguine may prefer groups and fellowship (being extraverted), while the phlegmatic tends to prefer the traditional and the formulaic.

MELANCHOLIC/MELANCHOLIC

You will relate in terms of truth, justice, ideals, order, space, and principles. You will both seek high ideals for the relationship and strive for deep intimacy. You will make a strong commitment. You will be trustworthy and dedicated. You will be very sensitive and giving, although at times you both can be overly sensitive to apparent slights. Watch out for becoming overly cautious and too inwardly directed, with neither spouse initiating fun or adventure.

Learn how to encourage friendships rather than engaging in pity parties or critical gossip sessions together. Learn together how not to globalize worries. You will both need to take time to talk and express your deepest feelings — not just in terms of ideals and principles, but how you really feel. You will have to draw each other out, asking each other's opinions and advice. Make sure you regularly express your appreciation for each other. Both of you are hesitant to ask for what you need and can withdraw instead. Remember, your spouse is not a mind-reader!

Overcome the melancholic tendency to express only critical thoughts while forgetting to compliment others. Focus on *self-giving* instead of becoming self-absorbed. Learn forgiveness through developing your interior life. Melancholic parents have a tendency to be very protective, cautious, and critical, and to make mountains out of molehills. Learn to focus on relationship-building with your children and not just sermonizing and admonishing.

PHLEGMATIC/MELANCHOLIC

You are both introverted and appreciate the private moments in life. The melancholic places a high value on intimacy (although not necessarily physical). The melancholic will analyze the relationship, while the phlegmatic seems not to care. The melancholic will want to talk about it, while the phlegmatic may just want to watch TV. The two of you will need to learn how to have fun. Go to a restaurant and talk, satisfying the melancholic's desire for intimacy and romance, while not nagging the phlegmatic. Marriage should not just be about duty and principles, but also needs to have those carefree moments of fun and frivolity.

You are both introverts, and you will have to learn to express your feelings in positive ways. Melancholics tend to criticize and globalize disaster, but phlegmatics are not motivated by criticism and will withdraw. Don't nag; it will build up resentment in phlegmatics. Don't lecture; they will tune you out. Don't expect your spouse to read your mind. If you want flowers, ask for them. Melancholics think that if phlegmatics don't know what is going on in their mind, they don't care, but melancholics also don't give credit to phlegmatics for always "being there."

Both temperaments can tend toward laziness, or can feel awkward about initiating fun and social activities. Both might be hesitant to initiate or express positive emotions and feelings. Be overt in your appreciation of each other. The melancholic should learn to pick the important battles, avoid negativity (which discourages the phlegmatic), and give constant, gentle reminders when the phlegmatic is not responding. Ask him what he thinks, or you might never find out. Compliment and make appreciative comments a lot more than you'd think necessary.

PHLEGMATIC/PHLEGMATIC

This is not a typical combination for marriage partners, unless at least one of the spouses has a strong secondary temperament. But if you and your spouse are phlegmatics, you will find that you both appreciate cooperation, peace, and harmony. You appreciate routine, order, and calmness. You are both patient and easy-going. You are tolerant, accepting of annoyances, do not dwell on grievances, and rarely engage in power struggles. You value commitment.

But, because you are so relaxed, you may find it difficult for one partner to exert strong leadership. Discussing difficult topics (which will inevitably arise in a marriage) will be a struggle, and you might want to avoid it, because you are both sensitive and averse to conflict. Both take conflict too personally. So both are indirect and may not be comfortable initiating, and that can become boring. Set goals and prioritize so that conflict avoidance doesn't lead to sweeping problems under the rug. Laziness and procrastination are often a temptation with this temperament. You may become a boring couple — reluctant, uninvolved, averse to risk and change. Strive for big goals to counter this. Keep focused and on track. Pay extra attention to diet and fitness.

You probably prefer structured environments; but too much duty may take the fun out of a marriage. Try to schedule special times for special occasions such as anniversaries, birthdays, and romantic getaways. Seek out ways to include openness, disclosure, fun, and passion in your marriage. Structured and planned getaways might offer this opportunity. Don't be moody, or avoid difficult situations because you don't feel like facing them.

Chapter 6

∽

Understanding Your Child's Temperament

"Love contains the acknowledgment of
the personal dignity of the other, and of
his or her absolute uniqueness."

John Paul II, Letter to Families

"Fathers, do not provoke your children
to anger, but bring them up in the
discipline and instruction of the Lord."

Ephesians 6:1-4

"Each child is a unique and unrepeatable person
and must receive individualized formation."

Pontifical Council for the Family

∽

A wise mother of ten once said, "When it gets to the point where you are yelling at your kids, you know you have lost control." Yet, how often do we find ourselves yelling, nagging, threatening, or even begging to gain compliance from our children? Sometimes it seems as if we approach parenting as an inevitable agony, or even an all-out war — complete with tactical maneuvers, outwitting the enemy, and taking prisoners.

What we really desire is for our kids to *want* to do the right thing, out of love and respect for God and for others. We know that one day they will be on their own, without parental guidance, and we hope that we will have raised them to be mature, loving, and generous Christians.

The axiom "grace builds upon nature" is particularly applicable to the raising of children. Pope John Paul II writes in his *Letter to Families*, "In God's plan the family is in many ways the first school of how to be human." As parents, we provide not only the material necessities of our children, but also the education and formation that will allow them to reach Christian maturity. Within the family, our children are formed both humanly and spiritually.

Yet how often the wonder and beauty — the *adventure* — of our sacramental role as parents becomes obscured by the day-to-day necessity of managing chaos. We find ourselves running from school to extracurricular activities, shopping and paying bills, working both in and outside of the home, and dealing with the myriad stresses of life. We can sometimes become so caught up in the "urgent" that we forget the "important."

One melancholic mom told me the following story. She had just finished cleaning the house when her adolescent son, home from a baseball game, came bursting through the front door — wearing his muddy cleats! She immediately chastised him: "*Look what you have done* to my nice, clean floor! *How many times* have I told you not to wear your cleats in the house!" She saw the light go out of his eyes, his shoulders begin to sag, and all the joy leave his face. He dejectedly went back outside, mumbling that she didn't even care that he had finally gotten his first hit of the season.

The relationship between this mom and her boy will take longer to repair than the dirty floor. The joy that he had felt at that moment and had wanted to share with his mom will never be recaptured in the same way.

An understanding of the temperaments helped my friend realize that a better response would be to show delicate restraint when her impulsive sanguine child burst in with the latest news, and to quell her own melancholic urge to focus on the offending details at the expense of the bigger picture.

The many books available on child-rearing, as well as advice from priests, educators, and loved ones, don't always prepare us for the reality and the immensity of our task as parents. The grace of the sacrament of marriage and the fruit of our daily prayer help us embrace this monumental task joyfully. But it doesn't hurt to have a few tools in the parenting toolbox.

One of the best tools is to understand the temperaments of our children. This is the key to understanding their personality, and it gives us a handle on how to motivate them, how to express our appreciation, how not to let our buttons get pushed — in short, how to show our love for them in a way that encourages and motivates them, and helps them grow closer to God.

By understanding and appreciating our children's temperaments, we are helping to form and teach our children within an atmosphere of love and respect for each child's uniqueness, thus creating a home environment that enables each individual to "fully find himself" in the sincere gift of self.[17]

∞

The atmosphere of the home
As you will discover, we strongly advocate that parents shower their kids — of all temperaments — with attention, affection, words of affirmation, and approval. John Paul II told us that the atmosphere of the home must be one of *acceptance, love, and esteem.*[18] Within such an atmosphere, children are more receptive and capable of learning virtue, and they blossom within the structure we provide for them.

We are not advocating a philosophy of indulgence or notorious "self-esteem" inflation. Unconditional acceptance in the absence of all structure or parental control merely gives rise to chaos and moral

SELF-TALK THAT PARENTS MUST CHALLENGE IN THEIR KIDS

Choleric child: My self-worth is based on what I accomplish; I have no self-esteem outside of my projects.

Melancholic child: My self-esteem is based on meeting my high expectations; self-doubt means I am humble.

Sanguine child: I must be fine: lots of people like me; my self-worth depends on what you think of me; I will adapt myself to the group.

Phlegmatic child: I'd rather give up my own desires/be alone/be unhappy than be in the midst of conflict.

[17]John Paul II, *Letter to Families*, 11.
[18]John Paul II, *Familiaris Consortio*, 26.

uncertainty. Children raised in the absence of structure are often anxious and vulnerable to social influences, or inappropriately take on the role of the parent in social interactions.

However, as the Pontifical Council for the Family emphasizes, the "affective atmosphere that reigns in the family" is "decisive."[19] Attention, affection, and approval help create this positive atmosphere of acceptance, love, and esteem. This atmosphere acknowledges our children's inherent dignity and personal freedom and fosters mutual respect[20] and appreciation, which, in turn, enable growth in virtue and self-giving. Within such a context, our children will more readily exercise their freedom to choose the *true* good. They will be far less inclined to exercise a false freedom in rebellion. They will be less likely to seek affirmation from unsavory peers who offer them a pseudo-affection, love, and esteem.

∽

Working with your child's temperament
When you fully understand the temperaments, you can work *with* the temperament of your child, and thus more easily direct him along the right path. For example, you can direct your melancholic child's propensity to reflection toward literature, art, and music. Direct the choleric child along the path of leadership — for a good and noble cause. Allow the cheerful radiance of the

---

[19] Pontifical Council for the Family, *The Truth and Meaning of Human Sexuality*, 50.

[20] Monsignor Giussani says that, etymologically, to *respect* means "to look at what is before you and perceive another presence" (*The Risk of Education* [New York: Crossroad Publishing, 1995]). When we see our children, we should also see Christ — Christ in them, and what He sees in them: their true freedom and ultimate potential.

sanguine child to bring joy to your life. Encourage your phlegmatic to bring his easy-going diplomacy to student government.

In addition to giving us a key to motivating our children, understanding the temperaments also helps us avoid pitfalls in parenting and gives us some insight into problems our children might be facing. For example, you can be cautious in making a direct criticism of your phlegmatic or melancholic because you know this will make him withdraw or become moody and less likely to listen or to follow through. You can see to it that your phlegmatic child is gradually given opportunities to initiate activities and to reveal what is going on inside him. You will know to refrain from attempting to control all areas of a choleric child's life, while at the same time directing his will toward constructive, healthy challenges. You will want to direct your sanguine's enthusiasm toward perseverance and constancy in the important areas of his life.

We have already discussed the temperaments in such a way that you can understand yourself better. Now we will address the highlights of the different temperaments in children. Finally, we will propose a way to better understand parent-child temperament combinations.

YOUR CHOLERIC CHILD
"The Dynamo"

The dining room table was covered with crayons, glitter, glue, and paper, and the floor underneath was awash in paper scraps and tiny beads. Our family was just getting ready to eat. "Look at the mess you made!" I cried. "I didn't do it!" insisted Lucy. I had to call her over and ask her to look at the incriminating pile of evidence. Her siblings stood by, amazed by her stubbornness even when faced with all the evidence. "Well, I was making cards. I didn't *know* I was making a *mess,*" she grudgingly admitted.

True to his temperament, the choleric child is a leader and a tightly coiled bundle of ambition: strong-willed, determined, a quick learner. He won't be content just to make the team; he'll want to be the leading scorer and take the last-minute winning shot. Because he has the ability to focus his will, and is very goal-oriented, he tends to do the things he likes very well. He is comfortable expressing himself and excelling.

The other side of the coin is that he can be rather impatient, argumentative, stubborn, interruptive, quick-tempered, and occasionally lacking in empathy — especially when things aren't going his way. You may have to convince him that the things he finds uninteresting may also be important and deserving of his attention: cleaning his room, practicing his music lessons, learning his math facts, being considerate of other people's feelings, or saying his daily prayers.

We realized that our darling baby with the bouncy curls and the big brown eyes was a choleric like her mom when we discovered that it was nearly impossible for her to admit when she was wrong, even when the evidence was piling up. The words, "You are right, and I am wrong" are nearly impossible for a choleric to utter. When "I don't want to talk about it anymore" or plugging the ears is not permitted and an apology is required, the choleric child might attempt a halfhearted euphemism: "I guess *you* think you're right," or "I didn't *mean* to hurt your feelings," or "I didn't *intend* to do that."

"Did not"-"Did so" arguments will continue indefinitely unless someone — not the choleric — gives up; perhaps the peaceful phlegmatic will let the choleric have his way, or the sanguine will throw up his hands in disgust. The melancholic will occasionally storm off to brood in her room, after pronouncing a decisively devastating recrimination. Power struggles are more likely with cholerics, because they have a more focused (if not always stronger) will. Nonetheless, power struggles are never inevitable — even with toddlers and teens. Since cholerics appreciate real responsibility, you can encourage your choleric child to be a part of the *solution*. Solicit his recommendations about how to resolve the current problem, and let him know you will consider his input — even though the ultimate decision is yours. Explain your reasons, encourage his cooperation, and generally it will come.

The choleric child loves to argue and debate. Don't take it personally. It's not necessarily a sign of disrespect or of willful provocation. Especially when they are teens — and still developing their powers of critical analysis and discernment — they may dispassionately take the opposing view to yours simply *for the sake of argument*. Reacting punitively to this contentiousness will only solidify their opposing stance. Tell your choleric child that, so long as he expresses his argument in a respectful tone, you will be willing to listen — even when you disagree. The fact that you are willing to listen to his arguments does mean you accept his position. You, the parent, always retain the final authority in all decision-making. However, when you permit the discussion of ideas, and listen respectfully to their opinion, even if you don't agree with it,[21] they will eventually turn to some other topic to debate and will be less likely to escalate the disagreement into a fight or a power struggle.

Young cholerics enjoy verbal sparring like puppies enjoy playing fetch. It is more a matter of sport than some attempt to usurp your authority. They want to hear rational, well-thought-out reasons for what you are asking them to believe or to do. The strong will of the choleric is one of their natural strengths; parents should never try to "break" it, but rather, should direct it properly. Our children will need great willpower to pursue a path of righteousness in the face of great challenges from negative peers and contemporary society. Do not insult their intelligence. Injustice; irrational, emotionally based, or corporal punishments; or an inability to give reasons for your decisions may diminish a choleric's respect for you. Teach them the difference between a respectful debate and a fight. Listen to their reasons, and ask them to hear yours.

The choleric child will be persuaded more by solid reasoning than by harsh commands; the latter tends to drive them to bullheaded resistance. "Because I said so," will not suffice; reasons are always required. "I shouldn't have to explain myself! I am the parent!" is what many parents say when dealing with choleric children. However, giving our own reasons is a small price to pay for fostering their intelligence and teaching them how to argue civilly. Besides, just because you have listened to their arguments does not mean that you abdicate your authority to make the final decision.

[21] Even when parents find their views childish or foolish, they should listen with an empathic ear and encourage careful reflection. But they must never use derision as a means to show them that their opinion is wrong.

Try to accept graciously the fact that it truly pains your choleric child to admit being wrong. Help him save face, while gently teaching the virtue of humility. Mention all the other times he was right on target; this must be the first time he is mistaken. Keep your sense of humor. Remember, this child may be a future lawyer who will be able to support you in your old age. Remind yourself that the ability to say no and to think things through for himself will come as a boon when he is a teen and is faced with temptations to "go along with the crowd" or to drink or do drugs. Once your choleric commits to a course of action, he will resolutely carry out the plan; and if he has a strong will to do the good, he will be a leader among his peers and a champion for the truth.

ℝ

To get cooperation, challenge

Your choleric child needs to be *supportively* challenged in order to find motivation. If you are having trouble motivating a choleric, simply offer a challenge: *You are really a fast worker! Let's see whether you can clean up this room in less than ten minutes!* In school, your choleric needs to be challenged by a teacher he respects. He probably wants to accomplish a great many things and will want to discover many areas in which to develop his talents. Work with him to choose the best activities and pursuits. So long as he is part of the process, he will feel that he is somewhat "in control" and will learn from your example how to make good decisions.

If you have a choleric child, do not deprive him of competition, challenges, debates, leadership opportunities, and ways to stretch himself, even if these things do not appeal to you, or else he may become bored or discouraged. It is vital that you realize that the choleric needs to have a sense of autonomy. If you, the parent, offer no appropriate opportunities for your choleric child to take charge and be in control, he make seek alternative, possibly self-destructive, means for taking control. Cholerics need healthy, uplifting, meaningful situations in which to exercise their leadership qualities. Pseudo-decision-making will not suffice.[22]

∞

Educating for freedom

Every child needs to grow gradually in self-mastery and individuation, these being fundamental aspects of human development and expressions of that beautiful gift from God: free will.[23] Overbearing and controlling parenting is never optimal, but it is especially deleterious to the choleric, who needs areas in which to exercise genuine personal control. The choleric will react particularly negatively to an overabundance of authoritarian control, especially in the absence of affirmation. They are likely to rebel — overtly or covertly. Authoritative (rather than authoritarian) parenting provides order and structure in a positive and supportive environment. Authoritarian and controlling parents tend to incite either rebellion or subservience — neither of which is desirable. Rebellion is the exercise of a false freedom (true freedom is

---

[22]Underlying this need is the genuine need for all human persons to feel that they are free — free to choose the right thing. When parents want to control all aspects of their children (including how they think or feel), they risk making "freedom" a bargaining chip; when free will cannot be appropriately expressed, even an inappropriate expression will do. Thus we find teens who run away, dye their hair purple, or choose bad friends to express a false "freedom."

[23]"By free will one shapes one's own life. Human freedom is a force for growth and maturity in truth and goodness" (*Catechism of the Catholic Church [CCC]*, 1731).

freedom to choose the good), and subservience is a denial of one's personal dignity and free will.

Compassion, meekness, and forgiveness are key virtues to teach your choleric child. Cholerics are natural leaders, but they need your help in learning the subtleties of interpersonal relationships. They need to learn to let other, more thoughtful children have a chance to speak. They need to learn not to interrupt or always to speak for everyone else. Teach your choleric child the wisdom of waiting — perhaps for days — before retaliating when he believes he has been wronged. Not every wrong needs to be avenged. Not every opinion needs to be expressed. Help your choleric child to appreciate the mystery and depth of other people — and himself. You may have to do some coaching: *I understand your point. What was going on inside you when that happened? How do you think others felt when you said that?* These lessons will help your choleric child learn to value the interior world of interpersonal relationships, without making more enemies than necessary.

The choleric child also needs to grow in empathy. Help him learn to put himself in the other person's shoes: *It's not easy to be team captain. If you show other players that you understand their situation, they will be more likely to listen to you.* Encourage him to become involved in spiritual and corporal works of mercy. Tutoring is a great activity for the choleric teen: it allows him to use his practical intelligence and to be "in charge," and yet also helps him grow in empathy and compassion. Encourage your choleric child to learn to express his feelings, so that anger and resentment do not build up. But be careful not to push him beyond what he feels is appropriate, for cholerics tend to loathe sharing their innermost feelings, even though they're extraverted about expressing their opinions. How do you encourage cholerics to explore their innermost feelings? Listen with warm appreciation when they do share an intimate moment. Show your appreciation for *who they are*, not only for what they think or what they accomplish.

Siblings and friends are important to choleric kids. But be careful when the young child complains of having been wronged; try to discern both sides of the story, for the choleric child is good at arguing and presenting his *own* side, but may not adequately understand how the other person was feeling. Young cholerics are likely to want to control whatever game is being played, and this will go over well with a phlegmatic friend, but when the playmate is equally strong-willed, sparks will fly. They can also hold grudges and will carry on a feud, with icy stares and cold shoulders, long after the other child has forgotten what happened.

If you are becoming frustrated with a strong-willed choleric child, it is sometimes helpful to remind yourself not to get caught up in secondary power struggles; whether the child is not doing what *you want*. Ultimately the goal is not to attain what you want, but to enable our children to do what *God wants*.[24]

∞

Leading the choleric child to Christ
When Laraine was in high school, her parents averted a potential spiritual disaster with prudence and wisdom — in a manner perfectly suited to her choleric temperament. A good friend of Laraine's had invited her to attend an entertaining evening with a

---

[24]Parents need to develop the virtue of patience, because we cannot always see the results of our (and our children's) efforts in the short run. "If we realize that it is a matter of achieving not so much what we want as of using the means available to enable our children to do what God wants, it will be easier to be patient": Cf. David Isaacs, *Character Building* (Dublin: Four Courts Press, 1984), 164.

Mormon youth group — just for fun. But one evening turned into two, and each successive evening became progressively more faith-focused until it culminated after several weeks in a hard-hitting demand that Laraine herself discern whether she was "called" to their faith. They told her that, if she was a "sincere seeker of the truth," she should read a passage from the Book of Mormon, and the Holy Spirit himself will convince her, by a direct sign, of its truth. When Laraine told her parents about this, they did not react hysterically, ban her from seeing the friend, throw the Book of Mormon in the trash, or lecture her. Instead, they made an appointment for Laraine to speak with their Catholic pastor — by herself. Father provided rational arguments and some background on the Mormon religion, and Laraine decided to spend no more time with that friend's youth group. To this day, when Mormon missionaries come to the door, Laraine can say truthfully that she has read that passage in the Book of Mormon and that the Holy Spirit himself convinced her that it was false.

Laraine's parents showed excellent parenting of a choleric. They supported her quest for the truth, refrained from an overly emotional outburst, and appealed to her rational side by initiating a mature step of speaking with a true authority. The pastor, in turn, was authoritative, rational, and ultimately persuasive.

In the spiritual realm, you will need to make sure that your choleric child is well challenged by authentic spiritual leaders and teachers who are able to give reasons for the Faith as well as motivate to apostolic action. Your choleric will be the first to sense any kind of phoniness or lack of intellectual toughness. He will appreciate a good theological debate and will want to defend his faith with intelligence. He will need to believe that the Faith makes sense and to be given ways to use his leadership skills in the Church. He will take to apologetics and missionary work quite naturally. But you may need to help him develop a personal relationship with Christ.

This personal relationship with Christ is critical for the choleric, to keep his faith centered on Christ and on serving him. In our foregoing example, Laraine as a choleric teen was easily lured because she was being offered friendship, a personal revelation from the Holy Spirit, and a spiritual *challenge*. The pastor offered personal attention, good arguments and reasons, and a greater challenge (to discover the truth). In the formation of conscience, the choleric will respect the development of reason in conformity to God's will.[25]

∞

Choleric children dos and don'ts

Do:

• Acknowledge their achievements and contributions.

• Give them opportunities to compete and debate.

• Give them good reasons for what you are asking.

• Pick your battles (or you will be arguing all the time).

• Help them to develop empathy and civility and to listen before speaking.

Don't:

• Punish them for arguing.

• Squelch competition and initiative.

[25]CCC, 1783.

• Control everything about their lives.

• Try to break their will.

• Take their arguments too personally — unless they are disrespectful.

YOUR MELANCHOLIC CHILD
"The Dreamer"

In every preschool class, there is one child who is contentedly playing by himself, a dreamy look in his eyes; a willowy sprite who is never boisterous, rarely makes eye contact with teachers (especially when those teachers are the cheerleader type). If the teacher is reading a story, however, the child will be all ears and can sit listening quietly for hours.

If you have a melancholic child, you are likely blessed with a delicate, spiritual, and often highly creative dreamer. This child needs to be gently encouraged to express and extend himself, and to develop a deep interior life.

Your melancholic child may seem to be not entirely "with it," but this is due to his deep inwardness and should be no cause for alarm (an alarm that may be felt more keenly by sanguine or choleric parents). No number of play dates will help; this is not an inability to socialize, for he enjoys his friends very much; it is rather an expression of his thoughtful, cautious, internal nature.

This child is slow to react, but the reaction will be intense and long-lasting when it comes. At first, he may not seem to react at all, but by the time his reaction is perceptible, it is already deep and nearly impossible to change. Take care, therefore, as the parent of such a child, not to drive a post of criticism, harshness, or resentment into this child's heart. You may not see his reaction externally, but the wound to the heart could later express itself in bitterness, rebellion, or depression.

Because the melancholic child's reactions are slow, a parent might mistakenly assume the child is not listening or is even willfully disobedient. To punish such a child for his temperamentally dull or slow reaction would be perceived by your melancholic child as the height of injustice. Fairness is critical to the melancholic child; principle and order are paramount. If this is abused by a family that wreaks havoc on the sensitive nature of the melancholic, he may experience long-term resentment. Perhaps the worst scenario for a melancholic child is to be treated unjustly, unfairly, and harshly on an ongoing basis. A melancholic friend of ours was raised in a highly dysfunctional family; treated badly by an unstable family member, she was told by her parents, "Life is tough; deal with it." This can have a traumatic impact on the sensitive melancholic's future relationships, his sense of personal self-worth, and even his ability to trust in God as a loving, protective father. A choleric or sanguine child might fight directly against the situation — whether verbally or by running away — but the melancholic child may internalize the injustice and even blame himself.

Your melancholic child might often find himself at the mercy of the playground bullies: his dreamy oblivion invites taunts, to which he is then unable to respond quickly. He may turn to his parents or to a teacher for protection, but this incurs further jibes as he becomes the dreaded tattletale.

It's a good idea for parents to give their melancholic child some tips on handling playground bullies; you can even practice these by role-playing. Don't just tell the non-athletic young boy to "toughen up and fight back" or expect the very sensitive dreamer to start rolling in the dirt and throwing punches, but some assertive language may help. Help him to understand that the bullies are not his friends and to develop a slightly more "carefree" attitude toward them (they tend not to pick on confident children), even a sense of humor about it (which shows that he doesn't care), while encouraging him to build strong friendships with other like-minded children.

∞

Help your melancholic child adjust to change
Because melancholics are slow to react and tend to worry, when introducing something new, it is always best to give your melancholic child fair warning and an opportunity to work through whatever fears or concerns might arise. With a sanguine child, you can say, "I've decided to move you to a new school," and (provided they aren't leaving two hundred best friends behind), he will look forward to the adventure and go with the flow. Your melancholic, on the other hand, will have a strong, push-back reaction to proposed change and will need plenty of time to adjust and to work up the courage to face the new situation. It is always helpful for you, the parent, to help him voice his inner fears and to walk him through the "worst-case scenarios" and his areas of ambivalence to help him see that it may not be as bad as he thinks or, if it is truly a bad situation, to help him find ways of coping.

Not only does your melancholic child need plenty of time to adjust to change or to a new idea, but he himself may never initiate change at all. As the parent of a melancholic, you will sometimes have to initiate change for him. By doing so, you will give your melancholic a kick-start, so to speak, and he will learn to self-adjust. For example, a number of years ago, our melancholic daughter wanted to try out for the school musical, but was terrified of the tryouts, and fretted and worried about them for days in advance. I knew she would love the whole experience, once she got started. So, I simply signed her up for tryouts myself, walked her to the classroom door, and then left. She handled herself with grace and aplomb, once she had gotten past the worry stage. Walking your child across the street to meet a new neighbor, setting up meetings with teachers or coaches, and kick-starting the college application process are examples of ways parents can help melancholics become successful. "Throw them in the water, and they will learn to swim" is sometimes the best advice for an irresolute, fretful melancholic.

Parenting a melancholic requires a strong will combined with a personal touch. Let's say your intelligent, melancholic daughter has a stack of college applications piled on her desk. As the deadline approaches, there is still no movement to fill any out. You, the parent, have a few options:

- *Do nothing.* You tell yourself that she needs to grow up, take responsibility for her own life, and if she doesn't fill out those applications, well, it's her funeral. But this option might work only with a very motivated choleric.

- *Engage the will.* You tell her in no uncertain terms that she is marching into that room and not coming out until those applications are filled out. This option might work with a motivated, but temporarily distracted choleric who steps up to challenges. It might even work with a compliant phlegmatic. But it will only drive the sensitive melancholic deeper into her inactive funk.

Melancholics will often see the importance of the task they are supposed to accomplish, but they are simply not ready to do so — out of fear or lack of confidence. Thus, option 3 is best:

- *Engage his will and use a personal touch* to get him ready for the job. It might sound like this: "Honey, let's sit down together and get started right now. I'll type at the computer, and you dictate to me how you want to fill out these forms." In other words, we help kick-start the melancholic, helping him to engage his will in the process and prevent procrastination. But we are using that delicate, personal touch that helps the melancholic feel secure and loved, and to come out of his shell.

∞

Teaching the melancholic

High ideals are critical to the melancholic, as well as plenty of space, quiet, and solitude. The melancholic is the most reflective and introverted of all the temperaments. Thus, a melancholic will need plenty of time to think things through or to process what he learned and experienced during the day. He will need a quiet and private space to "regroup" after a busy day at school or playing with other children. As a baby, our melancholic was sensitive to overstimulation and needed time to unwind before being able to get to sleep at night.

One mistake we made with our melancholic child was to think that she ought to be as outgoing and talkative as we were in social situations. We thought that her silence meant rudeness, when in fact it was her natural introversion and slowness to react. Our insistence on her talking and being "lively" only made matters worse and pushed her further into shyness. As she grew older, she became naturally more adept at social skills, and we realized that we shouldn't have pushed her so forcefully or tried to speak for her when she was younger.

On the other hand, the melancholic child *does* need to learn simple social skills, such as shaking someone's hand, saying *please* and *thank you,* and giving eye contact. Skills that come naturally to the extraverted sanguine will need to be taught to the introverted melancholic. When our children were quite young, we were visiting relatives, all adults, whom our kids were not familiar with. We prepped the melancholic and phlegmatic in advance: "When you meet Uncle Steve, I want you to look him in the eye, give him a firm handshake, and say, 'Hello.' " We even gave them some topics to talk about, so they would not be shyly staring at their feet the entire time. "Tell Auntie Anita about the book you just read." We didn't expect them to be witty conversationalists, but we did want them to meet certain minimum standards of social skills. Our extraverted children were always happy to hold their own in any repartee; our introverted children, on the other hand, were genuinely puzzled by the many questions their relatives or new acquaintances would ask them. Parents need to explain to their introverted children that adults often see lack of communication as unfriendliness or poor manners and that adults' persistence in asking questions is a sign of their affection and genuine interest in getting to know them.

Don't immediately try to solve all the problems that the melancholic child brings up. Often, melancholics simply want to be heard. If you try to solve all their problems, or, conversely, try to assure them "that's nothing to worry about," they may feel unappreciated, for coming to you with problems is their way of expressing their deepest self. Also, they may be deeply hurt by flippant remarks that a choleric or sanguine parent might make in an attempt to cheer them up. In fact, such remarks will have the opposite effect.

While it is important to be sensitive to the melancholic's worries or complaints, it is advisable not to overreact. A melancholic might complain about his teachers, yet still love school and get good grades. He may be upset and anxious about a work situation, yet still love the job. Remember that melancholics tend to complain more than other temperaments, and it doesn't necessarily mean that they want to give up.

One peculiarity about melancholics is they tire easily, and they show discouragement physically. The melancholic seems to need more sleep than most people do, and his body is sensitive; the fairytale "The Princess and the Pea" must have been about a melancholic. When a melancholic feels overwhelmed, he often thinks that what he needs is *more* sleep, *more* rest, *more* time to analyze the situation. But this can result in a cycle of lengthy deliberation in which he gets even more discouraged and overwhelmed. Help your melancholic stop this cycle by teaching him to articulate his priorities and discuss any ambivalence. Remember that melancholics need to think about important things; so help your child to articulate what *are* the important things in his life. Then, help him to engage his will to address those very things. While all children ought to attend to the priorities of life, this is especially true of the melancholic. If he finds that he is neglecting something vital, he will become upset and possibly discouraged over time. The more he actively faces the truly important things in his life, the happier the melancholic child will be.

∞

Young melancholics and the spiritual life
Because melancholics tend to fret about details, you will need to help your child keep his eye on the "big picture." A very sensitive melancholic may even find himself afflicted by scrupulosity. A male teacher at our Catholic high school used to discuss in detail the importance of fasting and penance. A mother of a sensitive melancholic girl told him that he had to be very careful, in today's climate, not to make fasting too alluring, for certain temperaments might take this to an extreme. Since then, he has downplayed fasting, especially with the girls. Melancholics need to keep in mind the overall goal — union with Christ — or else they may be tempted to focus all their attention on details or externals. (Should I genuflect or bow? Do I receive on the tongue or

in the hand? Did I fast for one hour, or was it fifty-six minutes?) This can result in self-criticism, discouragement, or scrupulosity. An understanding parent can help the melancholic focus on his relationship with Christ, his prayer life, and how his faith will help him attain happiness. The melancholic may be the most tempted to have a harsh image of God, so parents can help him see Christ as the one who "invites men to become, in the Holy Spirit, his adopted children and thus heirs of his blessed life."[26]

Young children, especially melancholics, will find the Rosary and a warm relationship with the Blessed Mother sources of peace and joy. The many beautiful Catholic traditions for the family are also a great comfort and source of joy for the melancholic child: making ornaments for the Jesse Tree, lighting Advent candles, blessing the home on Epiphany, baking lenten pretzels, and creating will all help draw him more closely to Christ. As soon as the child is capable, frequent reception of the sacraments, especially the Eucharist, will be greatly beneficial.

With a lot of support and gentle encouragement, and attention to good spiritual formation, your melancholic child will grow in "wisdom and grace," with high and noble ideals; a gift for recognizing truth, beauty, and justice; and a deep spirit and love for God.

∞

Melancholic children dos and don'ts

Do:

• Support them in developing initiative.

• Help them to see the big picture and the purpose of things.

[26]CCC, 1.

- Allow them introspective time.

- Encourage them to develop good social skills (e.g., eye contact, firm handshake).

- Give them a kick-start on difficult projects.

Don't:

- Punish them for shyness.

- Treat them harshly or unfairly.

- Allow them to isolate themselves.

- Match their negativity with yours.

Understanding Your Child's Temperament

YOUR SANGUINE CHILD
"A Star Is Born"

Sit back and enjoy a sanguine child! He is eager, bright, sensitive, funny, fun-loving, creative, and enthusiastic. He is a quick learner and equally quick to react, but never bears a grudge. He is eager to please others and wants everyone to be happy; fun is always a prime motivator. The sanguine child wears his heart on his sleeve: you will see in his expressive face the swift fluctuation of moods, emotions, ideas, and impulses.

As an infant, our sanguine child cried only out of sheer frustration at not being able to get out into the world and start partying. So long as he was in the middle of the action — in a backpack or in a walker — he was happy. His changing emotions were always evident on his face: crying one minute, gurgling and laughing the next. While this may be true to some degree with most babies, the sanguine child is distinguished by his expressiveness, his responsiveness to his environment, and his interaction with people. Our sanguine child used to draw stares when, sitting in a stroller at ten months, he would wave and say, "Hi" to those passing by.

∞

The sociable sanguine

One summer day at a swim meet, my friend Margie shared with me a difference between her two oldest girls, especially apparent when the two were on the same swim team. Her oldest daughter, a melancholic, loved to read and daydream. She would often just stand around at swim meets, feeling somewhat out of place in that highly vigorous physical and social environment. But her sanguine sister, two years her junior, immediately connected with all the girls her age and would be happily playing and laughing, cheering for her team, and swimming competitively.

In school, the sanguine child will learn most quickly when the teacher is animated, engages the kids with personal stories, and expresses his appreciation for them. Our sanguine son's favorite teacher (in whose class he achieved straight As) used storytelling to impart historical facts. Every historical event was tied to an anecdote — whether about the teacher himself or about some historical individual. This personal, engaging method of teaching appeals to most kids, but especially the sanguine child.

Sanguine children tend to have active senses and short attention spans; you may hear reports that they are not paying attention to their lessons; instead, they spend their time talking to friends or gazing around the classroom. A sanguine friend of ours relates that, in elementary school, she used to wonder why other kids were always looking down at their desks, writing.

The sanguine child *overtly* expresses his need for love and appreciation, certainly more so than children of other temperaments. In fact, a parent of a melancholic or phlegmatic has to be particularly attentive to this basic need in all children, because these introverted types may not let you, the parent, know how much they need your verbal and physical expressions of love. Even the extraverted choleric child will sometimes appear so self-sufficient that a parent might not realize how much physical touch and affectionate expressions he truly needs. Sanguines are, however, particularly expressive about their needs, their feelings, and their desires.

Your sanguine wants you, his beloved parent, to love what he loves and to spend time with him enjoying his pursuits. Our sanguine son makes the most of important "familial" occasions — such as the Super Bowl. He plans the menu, shops for supplies, and prepares hors d'oeuvres for the pre-game show. Everyone must be included. Everyone must enjoy the game. On one occasion, Art took Sam out on a special movie night, just the two of them. Sam became visibly saddened as Dad began criticizing the movie. He not only wanted to see the movie with Dad, but he wanted Dad to enjoy it as much as he did. A sanguine child not only wants to see a movie, watch the game, or go out to eat; he wants everyone to enjoy the movie, the game, and the dinner. Sanguines are hosts, not just participants.

When your sanguine is very young, you will have to be clear about limits and expectations, but try not to be repressive. The sanguine can easily become discouraged when a task or a rule seems to have no fun built in, or when he senses that the beloved parent is angry at him. Identify the important rules, and pick your battles. If you are overbearing all the time, your sanguine child will become discouraged. For example, when you want your young sanguine to go to Confession, don't try to inspire him with a dour "You have been really bad lately." Instead, try an upbeat "You will feel so great after Confession! And then we'll go out for ice cream to celebrate!"

Of course, if you are indecisive about your rules, he may take advantage of you. (When you say, "I'll think about it," your sanguine will often take this as a yes.) Sanguines need stimulation and activities and fun, but they also need structure and guidance, or they will try to get away with what they can — innocently, simply seeking fun, but this can be dangerous. So for sanguines above all children of other temperaments, make sure you know who their friends are, what they are watching on television, and where they are.

If you are a melancholic parent, however, you may have to remind yourself that friendships are indeed important; as John Paul II writes: "It must not be forgotten that reason, too, needs to be sustained in all its searching by trusting dialogue and sincere friendship."[27]

Parents and educators of sanguine children should strive to provide order and structure in the home and school environments, to counter the sanguine's natural tendency to inconstancy and disorder. Our sanguine child, for example, flourished in a structured school environment (in a school where he had many friends and activities), but floundered in a homeschooling environment, which is inherently less structured (and can be less social).

Provide your sanguine child with good intellectual and spiritual formation, so that he does not become superficial. Sanguines have bright, inquisitive minds, but tend to want to do the least amount of hard work possible, so they need close supervision in academics. But stay positive: when your sanguine child skims the surface of his studies or puts in a minimal effort on a project, you may be tempted to criticize his effort or come down hard on him. Remember, though, that sanguines personalize everything and will feel hurt when receiving sharp criticism. You will need to affirm his efforts (which to him *seemed* monumental) and, with your arm on his shoulder, personally walk him through the steps you want him to take, or make two cups of coffee and sit down with him as he studies, quizzing him before the major exam.

Without this guidance and structure, sanguines are prone to taking the path of least resistance — which usually is, coincidentally, the path of most fun! It is absolutely vital to teach your sanguine child to develop self-control and to reflect before he acts. Discipline is necessary for everyone's personal growth, but discipline does not come naturally to the carefree sanguine — especially sustained discipline. He will need your help in staying motivated

[27] John Paul II, *Fides et Ratio*, 33.

over the long haul. Help him to connect the dots between hard work and joy in achieving great results. But watch out for repressive, overly critical, rigid, dry, or impersonal instruction, whether in the human, religious, or academic realm. The sanguine child responds best to a patient, personal touch.

Memorization can be difficult and organization a challenge for sanguine kids. When your sanguine child is starting school, you may have to help him discover what inspires him to be organized and study hard: index cards with color-coded pens for memorizing, a planner with inspirational or funny quotes, special notebooks, and so forth. Work with him to develop a system. Don't just yell, "Why can't you remember anything?" when he comes home from school without his math book.

But, so long as his spiritual and intellectual formation is given in the context of a positive relationship, the sanguine is eager to learn. Sanguines need *cheerful guidance*, so that their butterfly-like natures won't lead them to disorganization, superficiality, and following the crowd. Give them an *attractive* goal to work toward, so that they can learn the value of hard work and discipline.

For example, one summer our sanguine son was preparing for a week away from home at a basketball camp that draws kids from around the country. Naturally, Sam wanted to have all the accouterments: new shoes, new shorts, and new shirts. Here was an opportunity to sit down with him and draw up a plan for earning the money he needed. During his weeks of hard work to earn the money, we made sure continually to praise his perseverance in working toward his goal. By our affirmation, we helped him connect the dots: hard work plus perseverance equals good things.

Sanguines aren't shy about expressing what they want. Instead of becoming irritated with their constant badgering about needs and desires, use those desires to set goals and to teach the value of hard work. The parent of a sanguine is like an athletic coach who channels the player's energy and talent, applying discipline, purpose, strategy, and order — not to kill the fun of the game, but to achieve success.

One wise mom of a sanguine college student keeps close tabs on his grades and checks in weekly, knowing the sanguine propensity to having an action-packed social life: "Are you drinking? Do you know your limits?" She is being prudent here, because to forbid him to drink would be impossible to enforce and might cause him to be deceitful. This way, she is able to keep the lines of communication open and uses her weekly opportunities to offer wisdom and advice.

∞

"Let the hearts of those who
seek the Lord rejoice" (Ps. 105:3)

Many times parents are tempted to say to their sanguine child, "It's time to get serious and buckle down! Wipe that smile off your face!" In forming the sanguine's faith, it is even more tempting because so much more is at stake: his eternal soul! Just remember that your sanguine is motivated by his love for you and for his friends, and by feeling connected and stimulated. When you tie these in with his faith, you can lead him to Christ. When you show him that he will be *happier* by doing the right thing, he will begin to understand. The Pontifical Council for the Family highlights some key factors in educating our children in the virtue of chastity — factors that are even more critical for the sanguine temperament:

[A] lack of interest in the children's education or excessive severity are factors that can cause emotional and affective disturbances in children. . . . Parents should learn how to listen carefully to their children, how to make the effort to understand them, and how to recognize the fragment of truth that may be present in some forms of rebellion.[28]

Friends are vitally important to the extraverted sanguine. Be sure to allow your sanguine to make friends — *good* friends who exhibit moral behavior and whose parents share critical values with you. True friendship combines charity and goodwill and helps children grow in virtue as well as human maturity. Having no friends is not an option. Christ had friends whom he loved dearly and with whom he spent relaxing evenings. When your sanguine child has wholesome friends, he will not need to seek to meet his affective needs elsewhere (in less desirable locations). You may have to help your sanguine at first to learn to identify which of his friends are his true friends and which are not.

When you further help him understand that Jesus is his best and truest friend, he will begin to want to please him. When you show him how constancy and perseverance in prayer has good results, he will begin to value these virtues. Show him cases from everyday life where good moral choices result in a good life, and where bad choices cause hurt and destruction. "God is truth" might appeal to the melancholic, but "God is love" and "God is good" will appeal to the sanguine. Make sure that he sees the example of a loving, merciful, kind father in his earthly father — which is the way he will first learn about his heavenly Father.

With spiritual formation, structure and discipline, and much love and appreciation, your sanguine child will bring enthusiasm

---

[28] Pontifical Council for the Family, *The Truth and Meaning of Human Sexuality*, 51.

and zest to all his endeavors and will bring joy and laughter to his loved ones.

∞

Sanguine children dos and don'ts

Do:

- Help them organize their time wisely.

- Provide structure and concrete guidelines.

- Give them noble ideals to pursue.

- Help them reflect and go into greater depth.

- Encourage them to develop good friendships.

- Communicate often, and appreciate their humor.

- Show interest in their friends and interests.

- Praise them when they persevere.

Don't:

- Take away their fun! (Don't be a wet blanket all the time!)

- Leave them entirely to their own devices.

- Deny them their social life.

- Scoff at their interests.

- Punish harshly or repressively.

YOUR PHLEGMATIC CHILD
"Future Diplomat"

Count your blessings for a phlegmatic child! He is a joy — so peaceful, quiet, cooperative, reliable, and obedient that you will be forever spoiled! He is quiet and cooperative in school and never gets into fights with other children. At home he can entertain himself for hours without requiring attention. If he is your first child, do not think all children will be like this, or get puffed up with pride in your own parenting skills.

However, you have to watch out. Your phlegmatic child can be so cooperative that you may realize, after living with him for ten or twelve years, that you really don't have a clue about what he really thinks or feels. What is his favorite show, or pastime? What angers him or frustrates him? What does he talk about with his best friend? Does he even *have* a best friend? If you are blessed with many children, you may end up ignoring the phlegmatic child; he simply goes unnoticed amid the bedlam of a large household. There he is, quietly playing in a corner with his Matchbox cars neatly arranged. He almost never causes problems, although he may be the one who takes all the blame and never complains, being intent on pleasing others and staying in the background.

The phlegmatic child is slow to react, quiet, thoughtful, self-controlled, and dutiful. He remains calm even under intense pressure. It takes a long time for anger to build in a phlegmatic. A little brother can annoy and provoke his older phlegmatic sister for days until finally, she will inform him, "You are so annoying!" and then become quiet and passive again. A phlegmatic's feelings run deep, but they are seldom expressed.

The phlegmatic tends to be so willing to please that he will gravitate toward whatever activities *other* people want to do. He perseveres in his duties out of a strong sense of cooperation and obligation — rarely, if ever, out of a desire to impress or influence others. So help your phlegmatic child discover what *he* really likes doing! Our dutiful phlegmatic son, a competitive swimmer, was training every single day, fifteen hours a week — including weekends at five in the morning — until one of us asked, "Gee, isn't this schedule rather grueling? Is it really worth it?" Only then did our son admit that he absolutely hated it!

The flip side to a quiet, pleasant nature is that, without proper encouragement, phlegmatic children can become sluggish or unmotivated. In new situations, they may lack initiative, taking a long time to become acclimated. Structured environments provided by certain types of schools or athletic programs can be of great assistance in providing motivation. You can also exhibit positive appreciation for their talents and their diplomatic skills. We encouraged our peaceful phlegmatic to run for student-body president, because (as we pointed out to him) he was respected by almost everyone in his class! He had virtually no enemies. He treated everyone — from the most studious intellectual to the most popular athlete — with equal respect and regard.

In the interest of simplifying life and decreasing potential work, phlegmatics will often defer to others important decisions that they should make themselves. They must be encouraged to make up their own minds. But it takes time to draw out what exactly is *in* their minds! For this reason, a phlegmatic child should not be rushed into making important decisions.

One day our phlegmatic son was feeling overwhelmed. His choleric mother was interrogating him about what colleges he was planning to apply to and demanding to know what steps he had taken thus far. Phlegmatic-melancholic Dad was gloomily lecturing on the Lack of Academic Motivation in the Youth of Today.

Our son's shoulders slumped, and his eyes began drooping sadly. Suddenly he brightened up. "I know," he said. "You just make me a list of my top three schools, and I will apply to them!" Our son was willing to *abdicate his own choice* in order to "make peace" with his parents, dispel the anxiety associated with contemplating an unknown and scary future, and avoid an onerous outlay of effort. Sometimes the phlegmatic will conform or surrender just to ensure peace, even if it is not in his best interest. It is never a good idea to let your phlegmatic child abdicate all effort and free choice. You may buy yourself some momentary "peace," but it will not teach your phlegmatic child how to make difficult decisions and to take charge of his own life.

This story is an example of a situation in which parental artistry is required when raising a phlegmatic child. Phlegmatics love peace and harmony as much as their parents do; but the kind of peace our son was after was really just the *absence of conflict* resulting from the path of least resistance, rather than the fruit of choosing the right thing and taking principled action. So, while it may be easier for parents to say, "Okay, I'll decide for you," it is not the best thing for the child. In this case, the better choice for us was to say, "Let's sit down together and discuss your interests and goals." And there begins the real work of mining the heart of your phlegmatic to discover his dreams and his deep desires. Help him make that extra effort to look into the future and into the depths of his own soul, and encourage him to find his passion.

∽

Help your phlegmatic stand up for himself

The phlegmatic may be introverted and slow to make friends, but friends are vitally important to him nonetheless. Phlegmatic children often learn by sharing in the interests of other children.

On his own, a phlegmatic child may not be intrigued by certain ideas or activities, but if his best friend is interested in a particular activity, he will be moved to try it out. It is, of course, important for all parents to know who their children's friends are. Because of his steady nature and natural aversion to conflict, the phlegmatic child is not as likely to be attracted by overly wild or provocative kids as the more impulsive sanguine might. Although extraverts will be attractive to your phlegmatic, he probably still won't want to "rock the boat" so much that he finds himself in risky situations or among a wild crowd of hooligans. If, however, the phlegmatic feels unaccepted and unappreciated at home, he may find himself attracted by unhealthy situations or by strong leaders who do appreciate him.

A very likely temptation for the phlegmatic is to take the easy way out, or to engage in activities that are easy and enjoyable, but divert energies away from more difficult, but more important, projects. For example, a phlegmatic who has put in several hours of work on a tough research project will feel that now it is time to relax — even if there is still work to be done! A melancholic or choleric will be likely to keep working until the job is satisfactorily completed. Phlegmatics feel entitled to rest and relaxation. A phlegmatic who is feeling particularly pressured to achieve academically, in the absence of a supportive way to handle academic struggles, might also be tempted to cheat.

You can help your phlegmatic child to come outside of himself by encouraging him to take on leadership roles. Although he may not seem like a self-starter, once you encourage him and remind him of his talents, he may become confident enough to try. With his thoughtful, reliable, and even-tempered personality, your phlegmatic can become — if he overcomes his natural distaste for conflict and taking charge — an excellent leader. His leadership style will be much different from that of a choleric; however, he will tend to lead by example, by serving, and by promoting cooperation from within the ranks. He will have a natural abhorrence for leaders who are showy, brash, and bossy.

The danger for phlegmatics is to become apathetic, dull, and slothful. If they are not encouraged — with much loving praise — they might never find their own talents, strengths, and interests. Worse, if they are ignored, nagged, or hounded, they will retreat into themselves, into passive activities like video games or television, becoming the ultimate couch potato.

Art once counseled a melancholic dad who was struggling to motivate his phlegmatic son. True to his melancholic nature, the dad would constantly lecture his son about what he should and should not do. This frustrated his son, who had a hard time expressing how it discouraged him to hear a stream of lectures from his dad after a long day of lectures at school! His grades were spiraling downward, and he withdrew from his dad; this caused his dad to lecture all the more.

Art encouraged the dad to make a 180-degree change in order to better show his love to his son. Art asked him to tell his son how much he appreciated him and to focus on his son's good nature, his cooperation, and his fairness. Art told him to shower his son with praise. This was not an easy assignment for a naturally critical melancholic, but the stakes were great enough to motivate him to try. By doing this, the melancholic dad was able to boost his son's confidence and to spur him on to action.

Such advice may seem simplistic; yet, it is surprising how few parents (especially parents who are introverted themselves) actually follow the prescription of giving praise and affirmation. It is all too easy to nag and criticize the slow-moving phlegmatic, until resentment has built up and he ossifies into a stubborn, immovable object. It is vital that parents head this off at the pass, by making sure that, for every critical comment they make, they have already given five affirming ones. It is our opinion that there are many great phlegmatics who have never reached their potential because of a lack of appropriate encouragement. These gentle and cautious souls need attention and many words of affirmation.

∞

Structured environments motivate the phlegmatic

Your phlegmatic child needs to develop planning skills: he isn't naturally inclined to look into the nebulous (and sometimes scary) fog of the future and imagine himself six months, one year, or five years hence. Phlegmatics are comfortable in the present and aren't given to grand schemes or dreams. Just recently we gave our two sons this thought problem: If we gave you a credit card and sent you to New York City for a week, what would you do? Within seconds, our sanguine son had an extensive list: a Yankee game, a shopping spree at the very first Nike store, a trip to Madison Square Garden, a Mets game. Our phlegmatic son said, "Gee, I don't know." These ideas don't roll off the top of an introvert's head. It doesn't mean there is nothing inside. In fact, when your phlegmatic is encouraged to penetrate the depths of his own psyche, you may be surprised by the maturity and balance of his thoughts.

Therefore, as parents, we must continually seek to uncover the depths of our phlegmatic child's heart and mind; with encouragement the ideas will come. We can reflect on the fifth mystery of the Rosary for our inspiration: Mary and Joseph had to search for Jesus for three days, wondering whether he was lost, kidnapped, or injured! Yet they found him exactly where he was supposed to be: teaching in the Temple: "Did you not know that I must be in my

Father's house?" (Luke 2:49). Mary and Joseph did not understand this. Often we do not understand the mysteries and depths of our own children, who have their own talents and gifts, and a unique mission from God. Like Mary, we can keep all these things in our hearts, and continue to bring our children to God.

The phlegmatic, perhaps more than any other temperament, benefits from a combination of structure, clearly defined expectations, and ongoing support and appreciation. The phlegmatic will need your help in setting and sticking to his goals. He is unlikely to complain, but equally unlikely to initiate. So you will have to help him find active areas of ministry, social clubs, and extracurricular activities within which his cooperative friendliness can flourish.

You will need to encourage him to grow spiritually. Teach him to see Jesus as the best friend of his soul and talk specifically about how he can strengthen his relationship with Christ. "That would please Jesus very much" will be a good motivator for the congenial phlegmatic. Teach him devotions and prayers that he will find reassuring at all points in his childhood. John Paul II tells a story about when he was ten or eleven years old and wasn't very enthusiastic or diligent about being a choirboy. His father told him he should pray more often to the Holy Spirit and taught him a special prayer. He prayed every day to the Holy Spirit, and he even wrote an encyclical on the Holy Spirit.[29]

Parents of phlegmatics also have to be expert motivators: encouraging their children to discover their own depths and passion. With good human and spiritual formation, the phlegmatic child will develop into an individual of noble ideals, exhibiting restraint

[29] Andre Frossard, *Portrait of John Paul II* (San Francisco: Ignatius Press, 1990), 74.

and self-control, and capable of making personal sacrifices for God and his fellow man.

∞

Phlegmatic children dos and don'ts

Do:

• Help them look to the future and plan for the long haul.

• Give gentle reminders, and make concrete, specific requests.

• Praise them for their cooperation, their good attitude, and their achievements.

• Encourage them to pursue long-range goals.

• Encourage them to develop social and leadership skills.

Don't:

• Ridicule.

• Nag or criticize harshly.

• Take over for them.

• Let them withdraw into isolation.

Chapter 7

Parenting and Parent/Child Combinations

"The family is in fact a community of persons
whose proper way of existing and living together
is communion: *communio personarum.*"

John Paul II, Letter to Families

"[C]hildren, while they are able to grow
'in wisdom and in stature, and in favor
with God and man,' offer their own precious
contribution to building up the family community
and even to the sanctification of their parents."

John Paul II, Familiaris Consortio, 26

"The best way to keep children home is
to make the home atmosphere pleasant —
and let the air out of the tires. "

Dorothy Parker

∞

Your child's temperament is a gift from God. You are the guide, the advocate, and the teacher who will help him make the most of this gift; to discover his talents and his true self. With your love and God's grace, he can reach his full potential. Your overall principle is to motivate patiently and lovingly, as Christ did with his disciples. Understand your child's temperament, work with him, and gently challenge him to grow. The sacrament of Marriage, which allows a man and a woman to share in God's creative action, also "consecrates" parents to educate and form their children in the Christian faith. We share in the authority and love of God the Father and Christ the Shepherd, as John Paul II wrote in *Familiaris Consortio*.

But while we teach our children and help them grow in holiness, they teach *us* and help *us* to grow. John Paul II said many times that we have much to learn from the youth. He told the young people many times at World Youth Day, "You are the salt of the earth. . . . You are the light of the world" (Matt. 5:13-14).

We will be better able to form — and be formed by — our children if we first learn how our temperament affects our parenting style and tendencies, and recognize the unique ways our temperament meshes with the different temperaments of our children. For there are sixteen parent/child temperament combinations, and each one offers its own pleasures, struggles, and challenges.

Before we look at those combinations, let us examine some of the typical traits of the choleric, melancholic, sanguine, and phlegmatic parent. Remember, as always, that these are "idealized types," and most of us are a combination of two temperaments.

THE CHOLERIC PARENT

The typical choleric parent is outgoing, of firm (and frequently stated) conviction, loyal, protective, and assertive. He is both an initiator and a motivator. He has high expectations for his children. He will be very comfortable taking command and starting confrontations. Usually, home life will be organized and run according to plan — the choleric's plan.

The downside is that a choleric parent can be overbearing, impatient, and dismissive. He may forget that the kids are, well, *kids*. If the choleric spouse is female, she has to watch out not to undermine her husband's leadership. If you're a choleric parent, you need to make a firm commitment to developing compassion, empathy, and tenderness — especially with very small, introverted, or timid children. You must be careful not to overwhelm them with your own forceful personality.

A very sensitive melancholic or phlegmatic might think that the choleric parent is angry or displeased when he is simply stating his opinion in typically forceful and energetic fashion. Once, our melancholic daughter was telling Laraine about a disagreement she had with some college friends about a point of faith. In typical choleric fashion, Laraine didn't wait to hear the end of the story before she launched into several heated arguments designed to decimate the opposing faction. When the diatribe was over, our daughter mildly observed, "That's one way to lose all your friends."

As a choleric, you may enthusiastically take to parenting: young minds to mold and to impart wisdom to! But watch out for creating a "boot camp" atmosphere in the home — especially if your children are not equally choleric. Special attention must be paid to the quieter children, and to developing awareness that family life is not all about "my way or the highway" (especially if you want your children to remain at home with you during their formative years!). Especially be on your guard not to give the impression that your children must have the same interests as you, be as assertive and outspoken as you are, or excel in every activity they undertake. This kind of intense pressure can be extremely damaging to a sensitive or quiet child or a child who is just learning a new skill; the child may begin to feel rejected and may come to believe that anything he does will not satisfy his parent. Do not allow choleric outbursts of impatience or anger extinguish the delicate flame of love.

THE SANGUINE PARENT

The sanguine parent is a big kid himself. He is playful, outgoing, adventurous, and truly enjoys his children. He is flexible and empathic: he sees things from the child's point of view. It's likely to be the sanguine mom who has all the kids in the neighborhood over at her house after school. The sanguine parent will be the one who creates "learning centers" in the basement, builds an elaborate jungle gym in the backyard, bakes cookies with the two-year-old, and takes all the kids and their friends to the movies. He loves to tell stories and get a laugh from his kids and their friends (and may mortify his shyer children with his antics). He is creative, accepting, enthusiastic, and involved. A melancholic parent will ask the sanguine parent: *How do you know all that stuff about your kids?*

On the downside, the sanguine parent needs to be reminded that children need discipline, order, and structure. He can be forgetful and inconsistent, and children may take advantage of this fact. He can also be talked out of sticking to a plan or following through on a tough program. A sanguine parent who homeschools may spend a lot of time doing science outside at the playground — while forgetting about spelling tests, math, and grammar. (After all, children need to *play!*)

As a sanguine who loves to be loved, you might find it difficult to set firm limits and to take an authoritative stance when your child has done something wrong. In these situations, your motto should be: "My child needs a *parent*, not another friend." Be careful, too, not to take your child's side against your spouse! As you set a positive example by motivating with joy and humor, work hard to develop consistency in discipline and a sense of proper authority in the home.

Parenting and Parent/Child Combinations

THE MELANCHOLIC PARENT

In a melancholic parent's home you will not stumble over Legos in the foyer or find dishes piled in the sink. At dinnertime, the kids will set the table, and the dishes will be put away immediately afterward. The house will be unusually quiet. A melancholic parent will keep the home beautiful and orderly, tidy and well run. The kids will be expected to take on a full set of chores, and they will be done properly.

This is because the melancholic parent is, like Mary Poppins, "practically perfect in every way." And he expects the rest of the family to be, too. Self-sacrificing, loyal, organized, detailed, analytical, and sensitive, the melancholic parent values high ideals — and wants these ideals to be exemplified in his family.

The principle of gradualism is particularly foreign to the melancholic, who wants the truth to be accepted and acted upon immediately — for the right thing to be done, in the right way, *now*. *Everyone should do as they ought. Why do I need to explain myself? Which part of "no" don't you understand?*

The melancholic, perhaps more than any other temperament, might have in mind a preconceived notion of how his children ought to behave, or what a "good child" is like. He might have more difficulty than the sanguine parent (who identifies with the child) or the choleric parent (who has a strong pragmatic sense) or the phlegmatic (who is quite simply accepting) in understanding the sensibilities of the child, in being encouraging, and in being *flexible*.

Indeed, if you are melancholic, watch out that you do not grow so attached to order and discipline, to your plans and ideals, that you become inflexible. This can be dispiriting for young children, who tend to cause chaos and wreak havoc wherever they go! Without a spirit of flexibility, you may become overly negative and critical, and eventually feel overwhelmed and depressed. Your children may take that opportunity to act out, or to challenge you. It is vital for you to remember that your relationship with your children is primary — that truth does not trump charity, but is the other side of the same coin.

Otherwise, your melancholic tendency to sweat all the details (especially the "small stuff") combined with your tendency to criticism and control can actually *cause* rebellion where there might not otherwise have been any, especially if the child is choleric or sanguine. In the case of a phlegmatic child, a lack of uplifting and overtly positive encouragement, combined with a tendency to negativity, can cause him to give up or adopt a defeatist attitude: *Why bother trying? I'll never measure up anyway.*

Don't assume that everyone knows how to be orderly; most children need to be taught this skill. Work *with* your children to teach them; don't just expect them to know what you want them to do and how to do it. Be patient with childishness; learn not to sweat the small stuff or take childish mistakes personally. Kids need many more compliments — expressions of appreciation and words of affirmation — than criticism. Make sure you fill their "love tank" before you make the critical comment!

THE PHLEGMATIC PARENT

Just as every parent loves having at least one phlegmatic child, every child would love to have one phlegmatic parent. He is calm, kind, patient, and gentle. He abhors conflict and is slow to anger. He values harmony, peace, and cooperation in the home. A good listener, he is also considerate, relaxed, and non-demanding. He is receptive to whatever his spouse and children have to say, empathic, and non-argumentative. Where the melancholic parent grounds the child who gets a C on an exam or is convinced that little Joey won't get into college because he isn't reading in kindergarten, the phlegmatic parent may not even notice that the report card came home.

The phlegmatic parent hates to confront, so it may fall to the melancholic spouse to teach the kids about the facts of life, or to the choleric spouse to march into the classroom and demand a parent-teacher meeting, or to the sanguine spouse to take Joey and his friends to play laser tag. The phlegmatic parent will help out if asked, but doesn't often initiate. He'd really rather put his feet up and relax. A phlegmatic who homeschools is likely to be the one taking a nap while the kids are supposedly doing their math.

As a phlegmatic parent, your tendency to minimize problems and guard the status quo can have a down side, too. Too much acceptance (without high expectations) can result in under-achievement — either by your children (who may not be encouraged to excel) or by you, for not providing enough opportunities for your family to grow and succeed. You should recognize that loving sometimes entails challenging.

You must be diligent in remaining positive, involved, and motivational for your children's sake. Make sure you're not always letting the other parent manage all the difficult situations or handle all the interpersonal activities. Go out of your way to initiate conversations and activities and develop intimacy with your children, or else you will appear distant, uninvolved, and uninterested. A strong faith and prayer life will keep you from becoming discouraged in these arduous (to you) tasks, and you will learn to become more active and involved with your children — to become a parent beloved not only for your gentle temper, but for helping your kids to grow and excel.

Parenting and Parent/Child Combinations

∞

Parent/child combinations

Every temperament combination between parent and child has its own special joys and troubles. Understanding the basic dynamics of your combinations will help you build stronger relationships with your kids. Let's take a look at a snapshot of each.

CHOLERIC PARENT/CHOLERIC CHILDREN

Extravert/extravert combination is good for communication and knowing what is going on. Let choleric children air their ideas and arguments; realize they are quick to react and speak before they think. Since neither one of you backs down from an argument, take care not to engage in useless arguments where neither will back down. Choleric children are competitive, so allow them to compete and learn to win. Give them opportunities to make decisions and to control. If they are right, tell them so and watch them beam.

SANGUINE PARENT/CHOLERIC CHILDREN

Good communication opportunities. Good opportunity to help the driven child to relax and have fun, too. Don't feel hurt if choleric children are argumentative; give them opportunities to compete and excel. Since cholerics are often intense, the sanguine can help them learn to be more sensitive to others and to enjoy themselves. Learn to set limits when they are small, stand firm, but pick your battles.

MELANCHOLIC PARENT/CHOLERIC CHILDREN

You will be able to relate on the level of ideals and principles. Don't take it personally when choleric children argue and debate. Don't punish by withdrawing when they blurt out something hurtful or argumentative. Don't be overly critical or they will dig in against your position. Show them that you're loyal to them first by defending them overtly when necessary. Some melancholics have a hard time expressing appreciation, but cholerics really need a lot of appreciation and special attention.

PHLEGMATIC PARENT/CHOLERIC CHILDREN

Your patience and tolerance can be helpful here. But do not assume choleric children as laid-back as you. Allow them to develop their many interests, and don't shelter them from competition and leadership opportunities. Don't take it personally when they argue and debate. Let them know when they are right; they always appreciate that. Help them to communicate in a respectful manner. Overcome the temptation to let them do whatever they want. Stay involved.

CHOLERIC PARENT/SANGUINE CHILDREN

Extravert/extravert is a good communication combination. Realize that sanguine children speak everything on their mind, but impressions are not long-lasting. Let them air their thoughts; be grateful for knowing what they think and feel! Make sure you allow for the sanguine child's need to have fun and just spend time with you (even though not "productively," in your choleric opinion).

Criticism wounds them deeply, although they are very forgiving. They need to feel appreciated and to have opportunities to be the center of attention.

SANGUINE PARENT/SANGUINE CHILDREN

You will have a lot of fun! Enjoy each other! Make time for good spiritual and intellectual formation for both of you. Don't let sanguine children get caught up in the superficial or faddish, and watch out for who their friends are and what television shows they are watching. When they are very small, be consistent in your demands, set limits, and create structure. Take an active interest in their academics and sports so that they can learn to persevere.

MELANCHOLIC PARENT/SANGUINE CHILDREN

Don't try to make your children be just like you. Know that they aren't perfectionists or driven by ideals, but are eager for relationships and fun. They want you to enjoy what they enjoy and have fun being with them. Stop lecturing and explaining everything. They are motivated by love and happiness. Help them explore deeper ideals and religion by connecting the higher level with joy and fun. Pick your battles. Understand that frivolous things like clothes are important to them. Don't squash their eagerness and joy through criticism.

PHLEGMATIC PARENT/SANGUINE CHILDREN

You probably both love harmony and peacefulness. But sanguine children want to have a lot of fun too, and that can seem trivial to the phlegmatic parent. Be sure to extend yourself to do special things and spend enjoyable time with sanguine children. Try not to give in to grumpy moods or to be too negative. That can ruin things for sanguine children. Go out of your way to compliment their enthusiasm, humor, and good nature. Don't just cart them to events; enjoy the events with them.

CHOLERIC PARENT/MELANCHOLIC CHILDREN

Watch out for your tendency to push your melancholic children to be more outgoing and productive. Allow them to blossom slowly and in their own manner. Be gentle. Be fair. Allow silence and creative time alone. Protect them from aggressive, hurtful playmates — go to bat for them — as the sensitive melancholic child can be deeply wounded. Help them with decision-making and with initiating change. Take the time to listen. Do not solve their problems for them, try to cheer them up, or cut them off by filling in the blanks, or they will retreat into themselves and feel unappreciated. Express verbal appreciation even if they do not seem to appreciate it themselves.

SANGUINE PARENT/MELANCHOLIC CHILDREN

Realize that melancholic children are introverted and deeply thoughtful. Don't rush them into activities or friendships. Don't try to make them be like you. Give them lots of space and time in which to communicate their inmost thoughts. Protect them from bullies. Allow them creative silence. Don't make fun of them or expect them to laugh at all your jokes. Don't take their moods too personally. Your enthusiasm can help them get started on projects and tasks. Just because they are rarely overtly appreciative, don't assume that they don't value your help.

MELANCHOLIC PARENT/MELANCHOLIC CHILDREN

You will relate on quiet, space, principles, and order. But take care that you both don't become overly cautious with no fun. Learn how to encourage friendships; don't get into pity parties or critical gossip sessions together. Learn together how not to global-ize worries. Help your children learn to express problems in a less critical manner. Learn forgiveness through developing a spiritual life. Melancholic parents have a tendency to make mountains out of molehills. Don't be too severe in punishment, or they will re-sent the injustice. They won't offer their opinion, but ask what they think, and you'll be impressed with the thought they put into things.

PHLEGMATIC PARENT/MELANCHOLIC CHILDREN

You are both introverted and appreciate the private moments in life. You may have to push yourself to be creative so that there is fun between you. Melancholics are generally principled so they have to understand the big picture when you give them directives. Both temperaments can tend toward laziness, or can feel awkward about initiating fun, so you may have to take the lead here. You both might be hesitant to initiate or express emotions or feelings; try hard to be overt in appreciation and attention. Remember their best moments, and tell them about them; brag about them to friends. Realize, though, they are unlikely to return the favor!

CHOLERIC PARENT/ PHLEGMATIC CHILDREN

Watch out for being too directive and driven. Phlegmatic children are more motivated by support and appreciation than by dares and challenges. With structure and support, they can be very competitive in sports, academics, and business. Help them set significant goals and to lay out the concrete steps needed to achieve them. Make suggestions, and give lots of praise and encouragement to motivate. Phlegmatic children need to develop their own interests, but will readily follow your lead. Learn to draw them out and take the time necessary to learn about their interior soul. You may have to confront laziness, self-centeredness, and distractibility. But lead with praise and support.

SANGUINE PARENT/ PHLEGMATIC CHILDREN

You will have to provide motivation and direction. Phlegmatic children are very inward and slow to express feelings, but you can connect with them on the importance of relationships. Help them to develop leadership abilities by giving positive attention and praise. Don't make fun of them, ever. Enjoy their dry wit. Because phlegmatics can be lazy, they might surrender to the energy of the sanguine parents and never initiate. Be patient but persistent in having them contribute and learn to lead. This requires great patience for the sanguine parent. Don't take their cautious or inward ways as a rejection. Both sanguines and phlegmatics can lose sight of goals and become distracted by the process; remind yourself and your children to set concrete goals and persevere in their achievement. Draw your phlegmatic children out of themselves with fun activities and your own sense of humor.

MELANCHOLIC PARENT/PHLEGMATIC CHILDREN

You are both introverts, and you will have to learn to express your feelings in a positive way. Phlegmatics are not motivated by criticism and will withdraw when faced with it. When you are "just pointing something out," they will take it as a crushing blow to their feelings. It will build up resentment in them. Do not nag! Do not lecture! Learn to pick the important battles and give constant, gentle reminders when they don't respond. They're easily wounded, so try not to intervene when you're angry. Ask them what they think, or you might never find out. Compliment and make appreciative comments a lot more than you would think necessary.

PHLEGMATIC PARENT/PHLEGMATIC CHILDREN

You both appreciate cooperation and harmony. It can be hard for you to confront your phlegmatic children because both you and they are sensitive and averse to conflict. You're both indirect and may not be comfortable initiating, and that can become boring. Laziness and procrastination are often a temptation with this temperament. Keep focused and on track. Look for structured environments. If your phlegmatic children deviate from a plan, confront them with praise and support to stay on task. This is often hard for a phlegmatic parent who is tempted to overlook most problems. Try not to be moody. Help your phlegmatic children to set high goals and to remain accountable — even when challenges and accountability are difficult for you.

Chapter 8

❧

How to Motivate Yourself and Others

"To motivate, then, means to call upon
values that attract and move a person."
Marcial Maciel, L.C.

"Make no small plans; for they have not
the power to stir men's blood."
Niccolo Machiavelli

"When an actor comes to me and wants
to discuss his character, I say, 'It's
in the script.' If he says, 'But what's
my motivation?' I say, 'Your salary.' "
Alfred Hitchcock

∾

The human person, created in the image of God, possesses both intellect and will. When our intellect perceives something as good or desirable, our will moves us to act to attain that good thing. The will, then, is the power of the soul that chooses the good.

But what impels the will to choose the good? Or to put it another way: what *motivates* us?

Love is the strongest motivator of the will; when a person loves something, he is moved, even driven, to attain it. If motivation is the fuel that drives the engine of the will, love is high-octane racing fuel. When you are in love, nothing seems impossible; even the most arduous tasks, if done out of love, seem easy.

If only we could work, pray, study, or exercise with the same passionate fervor and delight with which we pursue the things we love! But motivating ourselves to meet the less-exciting demands of our daily lives is a different story. As anyone who has ever made a New Year's resolution only to abandon it two weeks later knows, simply making a promise (for example, to lose weight) is not in itself sufficient to motivate us to accomplish a task. Nor is acknowledging what we *ought* to do and what is good for us always sufficient to motivate our will to *do it*. For most of us, there is an "execution gap" between knowing what we must do and actually doing it. If we could learn how to motivate ourselves better, we could begin to close that gap.

There is also the problem of motivating other people. Any sales manager will tell you that merely setting sales goals doesn't necessarily produce the desired effect. Any parent of a reticent teenage boy knows that if he doesn't want to talk about it, you can't pry it out of him. Anyone who has dragged a tired, screaming toddler from a grocery store knows that sometimes you can't get compliance just by demanding it!

Simply knowing what is right won't always move our wills to act. Orders, demands, and enticements alone are often not enough to move others. Human beings need *motivation.*

∞

"Just do it" is not enough

The inability to motivate ourselves and others is often at the root of conflict, whether between spouses, between parent and child, or on the job. When a wife complains that her husband never talks to her, could it be because she doesn't know how to *ask,* and tries to motivate him by nagging instead? When Dad resorts to yelling and grounding his teenager because he won't do his chores or homework, could the real solution lie in effectively motivating the teen? When the employee finally gets laid off because of his sub-par performance, could the boss be partly to blame for not motivating him?

You may object that a husband shouldn't have to be *told* to talk to his wife! Children should simply obey their parents without being told why. And employees need to do their jobs, period.

But this objection doesn't take into account *Original Sin.* Because of the fall of our first parents, our will is weakened and our intellect darkened. We are not always in control of our passions. In short, we don't always do what we should. As St. Paul wrote, "I do not do what I want, but what I hate" (Rom. 7:15). Until we arrive at the perfection of charity and obedience — which is to love our neighbor purely and to do God's will simply out of love for him — we will always be in need of some help in growing in virtue and in doing the right thing. Likewise, our loved ones — our children and spouses and others whom God has put into our lives — need motivational help from us.

In this chapter, we will see *how* best to motivate ourselves according to our temperament, and we will discover the right ways and the wrong ways to encourage ourselves, our spouse, and our kids to achieve natural and supernatural goals.

∞

"We must consider how to rouse one another to love and good works" (Heb. 10:24)

Temperament is a part of our God-given nature. Only Jesus Christ, the perfect man, had the perfect temperament (most likely the perfection of all four temperaments — with none of the weaknesses). But our temperaments are imperfect, with their own unique strengths and weaknesses. In this chapter on motivation, we will look at how we can capitalize on our strengths and minimize our weaknesses, to avoid those pitfalls that sap energy or decrease efficiency and effectiveness at work and in the home. Understanding our own impediments to setting goals and following through on them will help us not only in our work and at home, but also in our spiritual life.

This chapter will also help us understand how to work with the other temperaments — to learn the *right* way to encourage our spouse and the hot buttons to avoid; how to be supportive of our loved ones in helping them achieve their goals; and how to help our children grow and flourish. Every parent, educator, employer, or spouse needs to motivate as well as teach, explain, or request. "Therefore, encourage one another, and build one another up," writes St. Paul to the Thessalonians (Thess. 5:11). He goes on to tell us exactly how we can build each other up: "Admonish the idle, cheer the fainthearted, support the weak, be patient with all. See that no one returns evil for evil; rather always seek what is good for each other and for all" (Thess. 5:14). We will follow the example of St. Paul the motivator, who said, "I have become all things to all, to save at least some" (1 Cor. 9:22).

God gives each of us particular talents, designed to help us accomplish his will, grow in holiness, and attain union with him one day. God wants us to exercise our talents — not let them sit unused — and to be productive with them (cf. Matt. 25:14 ff.).

Not utilizing our skills and talents can be a major cause of discouragement, regret, sadness, and failed relationships. On the spiritual level, it can imperil our souls. We have a duty and an obligation to participate in the mission of the Church — in the apostolate — by our very baptism! As Pope John Paul II writes in *Christifideles Laici*, today it is more urgent than ever that each one of us goes to work in the vineyard, bringing Christ to souls and souls to Christ. It's part of working out our own salvation.

∽

Christ, the master motivator

Jesus Christ moved hearts and minds and drew them to the highest love possible, the love of God. In the Gospels, Jesus exhibits superb motivational skills. He simply says, "Follow me," and the fishermen leave their nets, their fish, their livelihood — and their father — in the boats and follow him immediately. These were simple, hard-working men whose families depended on their fishing business; yet, upon encountering Christ, they immediately leave their secure and predictable lives to embrace the unknown, to become "fishers of men."

When Jesus meets the Samaritan woman at the well, he seamlessly draws the woman from her desire for natural water to the supernatural thirst for holiness (John 4). Zacchaeus, upon receiving Christ's invitation, immediately announces that he will give half of his possessions to the poor and repay four times over anyone from whom he had extorted money (Luke 19:1-10). The Centurion recognizes Christ's leadership and true authority: "For I, too, am a person subject to authority, with soldiers subject to me. And I say to one, 'Go,' and he goes; and to another 'Come here,' and he comes . . ." (Luke 7:1-9).

When Christ called Simon Peter (Luke 5:1-11), Levi (Luke 5:27), and Zacchaeus (Luke 19:1-10), he was on the move, seeking them out. Just prior to the call of Simon Peter, the crowds at Capernaum tried to prevent him from leaving their town, but he said to them, "To the other towns also I must proclaim the good news of the Kingdom of God" (Luke 4:43). He was not a rabbi who sat in the synagogue all day and waited for pious folk to come to him. He was not an enigmatic spiritual master who waited on a mountaintop for disciples to appear. "He journeyed from one town and village to another, preaching and proclaiming the good news of the Kingdom of God" (Luke 8:1). Christ is not only transcendent God, but also the imminent friend who seeks us out.

"Could God go further in his stooping down, in his drawing near to man, thereby expanding the possibilities of our knowing him?" writes Pope John Paul II. "In truth, it seems that he has gone as far as possible. He could not go further. In a certain sense God has gone too far!"[30]

Jesus was accompanied by the Twelve, several women who had been cured, and "many others who provided for them out of their resources" (Luke 8:3). Prior to every call, he was out walking along

---

[30] John Paul II, *Crossing the Threshold of Hope* (New York: Knopf, 1994), 40.

the Sea of Galilee or visiting the people of the neighboring towns. Part of his ability to draw the disciples was the fact that he met them where they were: in their fishing boats, by the Sea of Galilee, in the towns, in their homes, passing through the dusty streets.

When Christ stood up to read from the scroll of Isaiah at the synagogue in Nazareth, "Today this scripture passage is fulfilled in your hearing," the eyes of the entire synagogue were riveted upon him; all "spoke highly of him and were amazed at the gracious words that came from his mouth" (Luke 4:16-22). He "spoke with authority," with graciousness and power. Later, when the followers of John the Baptist questioned whether he was the one they should follow, he said to them, "Go and tell John what you have seen and heard: the blind regain their sight, the lame walk, lepers are cleansed, the deaf hear, the dead are raised, the poor have the good news proclaimed to them" (Luke 7:22).

As the Pope likes to say, "Christ proposes." He invites, he calls, but he never forces our hand. To motivate, he uses authority (true authority, never merely raw power or control); he meets people where they are on the natural level, but he draws them to supernatural love of God; and he performs miracles of healing.

PRINCIPLES OF MOTIVATION

"If you treat an individual as he is, he will stay as he is,
but if you treat him as if he were what he ought to be,
he will become what he ought to be and could be."

Goethe

"Become what you are!"

John Paul II

Understanding motivation requires understanding change. When we are motivated, we change. When we lack motivation, it is often due to a fear of — or ambivalence toward — change.

Change, in turn, requires motivation. A child must be motivated to change from being sloppy to being neat, or from being distracted in class to paying attention. A spouse will require motivation to change from doing nothing around the house to helping out, or from being a mediocre employee to a superior one. An individual needs motivation to change from not exercising to pursuing fitness, or from overeating to practicing temperance. We must change in order to go from point A to point B, to go from being at rest to being in motion, and the impetus for change is *motivation*.

Thus, if we want to help motivate our children, our co-workers, our spouse, or ourselves, we first have to understand the principles of how the human person is motivated to change.

∞

Change, both natural and supernatural
Only God is perfect, immutable, unchanging. In God "there is no alteration or shadow caused by change" (James 1:18). Change implies the possibility of increase in perfection, but God is perfect. Yet we are imperfect creatures capable of improving or of

backsliding. Change is intrinsic to those of us who live in time and space, and we are changing constantly.

Steadiness is usually associated with strength. A person who holds steadfastly to the truth and to his principles, who does not blow like a weathervane in the direction of his changing whims, is considered a person of virtue. One who controls his capricious, changing emotions is a man of intelligence and reason. It was the wise man, after all, who built his house on rock (Matt. 7:24).

But flexibility is a virtue as well, and a person who is able to change when it is appropriate will be very successful. It's important to live by firm principles, but it's no virtue to be unable to change and adapt when the situation requires it, or to hold on to tiny details and incidentals as though they were essential. Being *adaptive* enables us to find ways of applying our core principles and beliefs in an effective way. Christ also calls us to change and to grow in holiness.

On the supernatural level, change means conversion — conviction of our need for salvation — which opens us up to God's grace. Conversion entails the daily effort to give ourselves over to God's love, to become the new man in Christ, to overcome the flesh, to rise to the spiritual level; a conversion of heart that does not cease with a simple resolution, but which moves toward action and affects our entire life.[31] As St. Paul writes to the Ephesians, "Put away the old self of your former way of life . . . and put on the new self, created in God's way in righteousness and holiness of truth (Eph. 4:22-24; see also Col. 3:10).

Our initial motivation for conversion can be something quite human and natural — such as the desire for healing or a material

---

[31]Cf. John Paul II, Post-Synodal Apostolic Exhortation *Reconciliation and Penance*, 4.

need — but over time we come to a higher motivation: contrition for our sins and love of God.

And lest it seem that we are like the Pelagians, who believed that this change can be accomplished by the strength of our own will alone (or by the cleverness of our motivational techniques), let us emphasize that although God created us with intellect and will and expects us to use them, nothing is possible without his grace! As Father Benedict Groeschel wrote, "Grace, combined with insight and choice, is the means of change."[32]

∞

Are you ready, willing, and able?

As we've seen, in order to change and grow — on the natural as well as on the supernatural level — it is not enough to know what our goals and priorities are. Knowing that we want to become a better parent or manager, or even to become a saint, is not enough to produce change. We also need motivation. Let's first examine just what we mean by motivation on the natural level.

Fats Domino sang about being "ready, willing, and able to rock and roll all night." Does Fats have a lesson for us? In their research, psychologists William Miller and Stephen Rollnick have discovered that Fats may indeed have been on to something. These are, indeed, the three critical components of motivation: in order to change, one must be "ready, willing, and able."[33] Let's look at them in a slightly different order.

---

[32] Benedict Groeschel, *Stumbling Blocks or Stepping Stones: Spiritual Answers to Psychological Questions* (Paulist Press: New York, 1987).

[33] William R. Miller and Stephen Rollnick, *Motivational Interviewing*, 2nd ed. (New York: The Guilford Press, 2002), 10 ff.

• *Willing.* Is the goal important to me? If it is not sufficiently important, I am not willing to change. Often, parents (and spouses) will nag their children (or spouse) in order to motivate them. This is usually an attempt to highlight the importance of change — which is necessary, but not sufficient, to initiate change. But nagging is usually not enough to create willingness where there was none before; in fact many people react quite aversely to it, and instead of changing or feeling encouraged, they find themselves enervated.

Does the following scenario sound familiar? Mom and Dad have been lecturing their seventeen-year-old son on buckling down, studying hard, and starting to look at colleges. Nothing is happening. The nagging begins. It might even escalate into threats of grounding. Often parents will lecture or nag to get a child to understand the *importance* of the goal and the importance of change. The child, however, seems to be quite satisfied with the status quo and does nothing. He thinks, perhaps, "I'm doing okay in my classes right now; I don't see why I need to change." He lacks what psychologists call *discrepancy*: an awareness of dissatisfaction with the present situation and of the potential for improvement. He doesn't realize that his behavior will not result in achieving his goals, and therefore that to achieve his goals requires change. A sense of discrepancy must arise from the individual himself; otherwise, he will just feel pressured to achieve someone else's goals and will not be *willing* to make a change.

• *Able.* Even when we do have a sense of discrepancy and are convinced of the importance of a change, we may not feel capable of achieving it. This will reduce our motivation, for who wants to be a failure? Smokers and dieters often feel pessimistic about being able to quit smoking or to lose weight. This lack of confidence negatively impacts their ability to change. It is a curious catch-22: when we try to motivate ourselves (or others) to make a change, we might emphasize the importance of the goal so much that it actually decreases our confidence in our ability to change! Thus we are left quite willing, but not *able* to change.

Confidence can be enhanced by a positive atmosphere of empathy and encouragement. That's why interpersonal interactions have proven to be critical in initiating change. Even a very brief counseling session can be just the right motivator for someone to kick his habit of smoking or to develop the confidence he needs to try for a new job. Yet the interactions must be *positive*. In helping another person feel confident to change, we must be empathic, warm, and genuine in our support.[34]

Research has shown that people will change when they feel understood and when others have confidence in their ability to change.[35] Empathic listening is an effective way to boost confidence and thus help encourage positive change. Empathy is not simply agreeing with a person or necessarily condoning his thoughts or feelings. Nor is it a simple matter of parroting another's words or expressions. Christ gave us the model for true empathy for, and radical intimacy with, another: out of love for us, he *became* one of us! "He emptied himself, taking the form of a slave" (Phil. 2:7).

Empathy is putting yourself in the other person's shoes. It involves a skilled listening that both clarifies and amplifies the other's experience in a non-threatening manner. It is radically interested

[34]Miller and Rollnick, *Motivational Interviewing*, 7. Miller and Rollnick cite their research which proved that empathy was a significant determinant in responsiveness to treatment. Conversely, confrontational treatment caused alcoholics to *increase* their drinking.

[35]Ibid., 9, 37 ff.

and radically respectful. An empathic response will not only hear what the other person is saying, but will demonstrate understanding. This level of understanding and respect will show the other person that we truly have his best interest at heart, and this will help motivate him to change.

• *Ready.* Sure, the goal is important to me, and I feel capable of attaining it, but am I willing and able to change *right now?* How often do we say instead, *I'll study, but not this minute. I'll lose weight — after the holidays. I'll have time in the summer to spend some quality time with the kids. It's important, and I'll do it. But just not right now.*

Readiness can be enhanced by working through ambivalence, by learning to prioritize goals, and by breaking down goals into interim steps that are more easily manageable — now. In the day-to-day, we often find ourselves almost mindlessly responding to the demands of the urgent: the ringing phone, the doorbell, the fretful child, the angry boss. If we take time to reflect upon what is truly important, and to prioritize the most important goals, we will be ready to make a significant change when such a goal calls for one.

∞

False motivators only inhibit change

Oftentimes, in a sincere attempt to motivate, people use threats, punishment, humiliation, intimidation, or other means of forcing people to change. Yet these techniques rarely work, precisely because they undermine an individual's confidence in his ability to change. Fear of pain or threat of punishment can have the opposite effect: immobilizing people, rendering them even less likely to change for the better.[36]

[36] Ibid., 12.

"Boot camp therapy" (pain, suffering, punishment) will not necessarily motivate! Drug addicts, alcoholics, and compulsive gamblers are some of the most change-resistant clients;[37] researchers have found that increasing the amount of suffering, pain, or humiliation these individuals are already undergoing does not by itself provoke change. These people are usually well aware of the importance of change, yet they remain ambivalent about changing. In these cases, constructive change will occur only when the individual sees *for himself* the importance of the change, and is helped by an empowering, supportive atmosphere to feel capable of changing.

Being told you are a slob doesn't inspire you to become neat as much as being assured that you have the organizational skills to become tidier. Controlling, ordering, and providing solutions for someone also can negatively impact an individual's ability to change, because these things decrease the sense of personal autonomy and responsibility — freedom — which is vital to motivation.

Trying to order or command someone to change imposes your view of what is important, instead of evoking the individual's own awareness of what is important. Your view may be the correct one, but the person won't be motivated until he sees it for himself. Of course, there are many occasions when commanding is appropriate (in the military, for example). But, it would be fruitless to use such means for every instance in which motivation is required.

---

[37]Ibid., 14. These individuals often see the importance of change, and want to change, but they are inexorably drawn to the addictive behavior. Miller and Rollnick assert that the ambivalence itself is not pathological, but a normal aspect of human nature, and that these individuals need to be educated in order to move beyond the ambivalence.

Furthermore, even in the military, there is a higher motivation that actually causes the soldier to obey his commander: his love for his country, and his desire to serve his country and defend freedom. People are motivated to change when they perceive the goal as intrinsically worthy, of great value, something cherished. Within a positive, constructive, accepting atmosphere they are able to find the confidence to be able to change.[38]

∞

How to motivate for spiritual change

The model of being "ready, willing, and able" also applies in the spiritual life, provided we humbly appreciate the absolute necessity of God's grace. It is a curious — but very human — phenomenon that, although our ultimate goal is to be united with God one day in heaven, we do not behave on a daily basis as though this were a priority. We all share St. Paul's lament in Romans 7:19: "I do not do what I want, but I do what I hate."

Anyone who has attended a retreat following St. Ignatius of Loyola's *Spiritual Exercises* will recall that the meditations of the first week are designed to help us enter into the mystery of sin and evil, and to experience a sense of our own sinfulness and the times we have rejected God's love. To stir up further the need for conversion, St. Ignatius offers a meditation on hell: we can imagine the fire and the burning souls of the damned, smell the putrid sulphurous stench, hear the howling and wailing and blasphemies. Until we face the certainty of our death and the fact that how we live now critically impacts our future eternal salvation or damnation, we will not make our spiritual life a priority. We will not be ready to take steps toward the perfection of our souls.

[38]Ibid., 12.

Through these meditations, we come face-to-face with that discrepancy between how we live our lives — the daily transgressions, the sins against charity, the sins of our past — and where we want to spend our eternity: in heaven. This discrepancy gives rise to the need for change on the spiritual level: for *conversion*. During the second week of the *Spiritual Exercises,* we meditate on the "two standards": Christ, our commander-in-chief, and Satan, our mortal enemy. We realize that we must make a choice; no one can serve two masters.

As we confront our own sinfulness and the many ways we reject God's love, we realize how truly unworthy we are, how humanly impossible it is to change our weak human nature and to grow in holiness so that we may approach the King! Yet "all things are possible for God" (Mark 10:27). Although we are unworthy, God so loves each one of us that he died for us. Even if I were the only person on earth, Jesus Christ would have suffered and died on the Cross to save me. When we consider this, we can slowly begin to have that true confidence which only comes from God, confidence that, with his grace, we, too, may grow in holiness and may one day be united with him.

St. Ignatius does not leave us with an overwhelming feeling of crushing sorrow and unworthiness; rather, he inspires us with hope. He brings us to an overflowing sense of love for God, who has done so much for us: What can we give him in return? Moved by love, St. Ignatius offers this prayer: "Take, Lord, and receive all my liberty, my memory, my intellect, and all my will — all that I have and possess. . . . Your love and your grace are enough for me."

Inspired by love, we become energized — ready, willing, and able — to share God's love with others, to put ourselves at the service of the Kingdom, and to fulfill our mission with joy and confidence.

The Temperament God Gave You

∞

Motivation and the temperaments

Now that we have a psychological framework on which to base our understanding of motivation, how can we apply this to our understanding of the different temperaments?

Some of the temperaments, at first glance, appear to be more self-motivated or more easily motivated than others. Others display weakness in particular aspects of motivation — in readiness, willingness, or ability. When we identify these particular areas of weakness, and understand how to strengthen each particular area, we will be far more capable of motivating ourselves and others. This will be a boon not only on the natural level, but also in our spiritual lives.

It seems clear that the choleric and sanguine temperaments are the most easily motivated — at least at the outset. There is no doubt that people with the quickest and strongest reactions will be most ready to change: the choleric and sanguine are almost always ready. In addition, both choleric and sanguine, with their confidence and optimism, will usually consider themselves able. Willingness, a matter of perceiving the importance of change, is usually quickly grasped by the pragmatic intellect of the choleric. The sanguine, too, with his openness and enthusiasm, often quickly grasps the importance of a particular venture or new idea and will be ready to run with it.

These temperaments are not without weaknesses, however, when it comes to motivation. The choleric can suffer from an overabundance of confidence, which can result in his minimizing the importance of change. ("I'm such a quick study, I don't need to read the directions; I can figure it out myself.") This confidence can also result in a failure to choose the *right* goal, to take direction, or to be a team player — again, impacting motivation to

174

change by denying its importance. This can be a serious flaw when it is reflected in the choleric's spiritual life.

The weakness of the sanguine is that, due to his heightened sensibilities, he is easily distracted from his goal, and will be quickly motivated — to pursue *another* goal, another bright star, another whim. The sanguine is often ready to change, but may lack the commitment and focus necessary to reach his goal. Lacking confidence in his ability to persevere to the end, the sanguine may be tempted to rationalize ("I don't really care about making the team") or to blame ("It's not my fault that I didn't get a good grade on the test; the teacher didn't explain it properly"). The sanguine must strive for perseverance.

Both the melancholic and phlegmatic temperaments tend to react slowly. The melancholic tends to place a greater emphasis on analysis and contemplation, and thus may never get around to action. He suffers from a lack of *readiness*. The intellect abhors action, and the melancholic relies greatly on the intellect. As a result, the melancholic temperament often needs a kick-start. More so than the other temperaments, the skeptical, analytical melancholic needs to be sold on the *importance* of the goal. Furthermore, his tendency to self-criticism can undermine his confidence — in himself and in others. Lacking confidence, the melancholic may procrastinate, resulting in a further decrease of motivation.

The phlegmatic, too, will suffer from lack of readiness. He may be initially hampered by a lack of confidence, which will impact his ability to make the changes necessary. In addition, the phlegmatic, with his adaptable and peaceful nature, is often too fond of overlooking any discrepancy; he therefore does not become aware of the importance of change. He seems too satisfied with the status quo, too willing to adapt in order to accommodate setbacks and failure, too ready to dismiss the need for change.

For this reason, the temptation to nag and push a phlegmatic is extremely high; it's an understandable attempt to heighten his sense of discrepancy, to make him aware of the importance of change, but nagging phlegmatics only makes them discouraged and fearful, lacking confidence that they can achieve their goal. They become even less motivated than they were before.

∞

The temperaments and
four keys to accomplishing goals

The phlegmatic may at first appear to be the least motivated of the four temperaments. But the truth is that each temperament faces its own unique motivation challenges. When it comes to setting and accomplishing goals successfully, there are four key areas to consider:

+ Setting the right goals.

+ Getting started.

+ Overcoming obstacles.

+ Persevering until the end.

Each of the four temperaments has a characteristic weakness in one of these four areas. Understanding how to strengthen these weaknesses will help anyone's motivation — from inconstant sanguines to scrupulous melancholics; from the most overly confident choleric to the most complacent phlegmatic.

MOTIVATING THE CHOLERIC
The challenge: Setting the right goals

As discussed earlier, the passionate choleric is a self-motivated leader, naturally driven to complete his objectives. His keen, pragmatic, intellect quickly assesses the steps necessary to achieve his goals and, once he sets his sights, he is off and running like the Energizer Bunny.

The key for the choleric is the first step: setting the proper goals. Because of his quickness, zeal, and strong will, the choleric may hastily and imprudently choose a goal that contains serious flaws. He tends not to seek advice, for he tends to overvalue his own intelligence and his assessment of the situation at hand. He may not have properly considered all of the surrounding issues and can be imprudent in his haste; then, out of pride, he refuses to reconsider or change course.

Thus, in terms of setting and achieving goals, the choleric should learn to take the time necessary to choose goals properly, identify the most prudent course of action, and listen to advice. The choleric may be tempted to do what he wants to do without stopping to reflect on whether it is the right or the most prudent thing to do, or whether it is what God wants him to do.

Our youngest daughter is choleric. Her brothers and sister call her bullheaded and stubborn. Getting her to switch tasks from the one she prefers working on (or the one she has decided to work on) to the less-preferred, but necessary, task can be challenging. If you merely demand compliance or threaten, she will simply dig in.

Try instead to present a challenge to the young choleric (*I'll bet you can't clean your room in just fifteen minutes!*) and always give reasons for your requests (*You will be able to concentrate better on*

The Temperament God Gave You

your homework if your desk is clean and organized). The choleric temperament enjoys a challenge or a competition, and always demands reasons.

> CHOLERIC
>
> **Motivational strengths:** Highly productive, naturally motivated, and persevering.
>
> **Weaknesses:** Tends to overlook details and can roll over people. Impatient with lack of results. Can be overly confident.
>
> **Challenges:** Needs to take more time to set the *right* goals and strategize to ensure that prudential decisions are made. Needs to be charitable in dealing with people along his path. Needs to reflect more on the details, and to be more open to good advice from others.

If you are a choleric and are undertaking a project, take the time to do your homework before you even begin. Make sure your judgments are well researched and prudential. Get advice from an expert (or a spiritual director). *Listen* to others' recommendations.

Once a choleric starts in on a project, he can be like a steamroller or a charging horse — with blinders on. Anyone between him and his goal should *watch out!* A choleric breadwinner can roll right over his family, hot in pursuit of a challenging workplace goal. A choleric mother can be found driving her kids to numerous after-school enrichment activities and running a home-based business — forgetting all about dinner! Choleric Laraine has often experienced the temptation to work on a goal that is more rewarding (such as writing a book) rather than a lesser, although at times equally important, goal (such as doing the laundry).

Choleric Richard complained that his wife didn't understand all the pressures he faced at work. She wanted him to cut back his work hours and spend more time with the family. He was in a position of great responsibility and felt he couldn't be successful at work if he cut back. Art acknowledged the bind he was in, but also challenged him: "Aren't your kids' basketball games important?" "Absolutely," he replied. "And are all your meetings at work equally important?" "Of course not," he replied. A true leader will be able to cut out some of the less important meetings at work or reschedule them so that he can attend to important family duties. "Truly great leaders are not only successful at work; they are also heroes at home, to their wife and kids," Art said. The point here is, rather than telling a choleric to cut back or lower his sights, challenge him to be *more* — more efficient, more familial, more generous. Challenging someone does not preclude being empathic; challenges without empathy can easily come across as anger — which is not at all motivating!

With regard to beginning the task, overcoming obstacles, and persevering until the end, cholerics are pros! Obstacles are often viewed as challenges and are put to rest decisively. Oftentimes, the choleric will be so decisive about handling an obstacle that he will neglect to look at all sides of the issue. He makes a decision, and the task is off the plate. However, cholerics sometimes are too hasty in their swiftness to put a task to rest. They can be wrong, although they will hate to admit this. They need to develop thoroughness in checking all the facts and caution in responding to objections, and they need to use this rule of thumb, especially with regard to decisions provoked out of anger: wait three days before taking decisive or retributive action.

The choleric may achieve many goals and overcome many obstacles, but, as St. Paul says, without love, he or she becomes a "resounding gong or a clashing symbol" (1 Cor. 13). The choleric needs to watch out that he does not violate charity when dealing with human "obstacles." All too often, the steamroller will roll right over people who are thought to be standing in the way of the goal.

As with all the temperaments, the choleric is tempted to assume that everyone else is motivated in the same way he is. One choleric coach we know assumed that all the team members were equally motivated by goals to achieve personal records or to score more points for the team than anyone else. But some of the kids on the team were actually motivated by team spirit and cheering on their friends, and felt encouraged when the coach said, "You really tried hard!" or "I appreciate that great effort you made." They became discouraged when all the focus was on time and points. The coach realized that by broadening his motivational repertoire, he could actually achieve greater success.

What happens when a choleric allows himself to be ruled by pride and anger, and is faced with contradiction or resistance to his objective? The choleric will take it personally and view it as extreme disloyalty; he can be harsh in retribution or in silencing or getting rid of an opponent. He might jump to conclusions and make unjust accusations against the offending party. Pride refuses to allow him to apologize or forgive; anger may even turn to hatred.

It is vital for cholerics to stay close to the sacraments, to maintain a strong prayer life, and to receive spiritual direction from a reliable source. It's all too

> **MOTIVATING COMMENTS FOR THE CHOLERIC**
>
> "Your idea is great!"
>
> "I think your plan will save the company, but let's make sure this is the right goal before we embark."
>
> "What does the rest of the team think about it?"
>
> "Let's brainstorm some ideas to avoid potential pitfalls."

easy for the choleric to become angry or impassioned about an issue or idea, to solve the problem or deal with the issue hastily and
imprudently, only to discover that the original information was
incorrect! By the time the choleric learns that he was not, in fact,
right about the issue, the damage has been done and other people
have been hurt.

∞
Key points for the choleric

◆ *Think it through!* Develop the virtue of prudence, which is
a virtue of both intellect and will — requiring intelligence
and action. Through prudence, we are able to make the
right choice and take the right action to attain our goals.
We can work toward developing this virtue by developing
patience and calmness in sizing up situations, by carefully
analyzing relevant information, and by measuring our options against true standards. Help children slow down, focus
attention, and make accurate observations. If we are grown-
ups, we should guard against hasty decisions!

◆ *Patience!* Things come fast and easy to a choleric. But
driving eighty miles per hour on a winding road is dangerous. Patience requires interior peace, sensitivity, and the
ability to control our reactions. Help your choleric child develop patience when he is young, by allowing him to develop his feelings, but to control them and by encouraging
sensitivity with regard to others.

◆ *Charity.* The choleric is not impressed by doing things
merely to be nice. But you can persuade him to consider
the importance of charity on the natural level in terms of

effectiveness in dealing with people (people will do more if they are motivated) and on the supernatural level, because Christ asked us to be perfect, even as our heavenly Father is perfect. God is love. There is no true success without love.

MOTIVATING THE MELANCHOLIC
The challenge: Getting started

The melancholic has a deeply reflective nature and will fix his sight on the highest and noblest of goals. Reflection is of great benefit in the proper setting of priorities and goals; however, the melancholic can dwell too long in introspection. Taking too many things into consideration, second-guessing, weighing all the possible consequences of an action, and reflecting on all potential difficulties often results in an inability to act decisively. Thus, the melancholic may appear irresolute, indecisive, and procrastinating.

Because the melancholic has high ideals and strives for perfection, establishing priorities and setting goals is critical. If he does not set his goals clearly, he may find himself a victim of uncertainty. When a melancholic does not take the time to reflect and meditate on the truly important things in life, especially from a spiritual perspective, he may end up making mountains out of molehills, and driving himself and those around him crazy by over-attention to lesser details.

Genevieve was just such a melancholic. Her marriage was becoming strained because of her tendency to lecture in a high-handed manner on all aspects of her children's and her husband's lives. From her perspective, she was just attending to all those important details a mom should attend to: homework, healthful food, and extracurricular activities for the kids — even their spiritual lives! She helped them say their prayers, took them all to Confession, and helped out at school and church. She watched out for her husband's career and monitored his list of networking contacts. She was judgmental when others didn't meet her standards; they began to dread her and to avoid her. She was driving everyone crazy in her home! Why? Her commitment was to perfection — the perfecting of her children and her spouse! Our goal should always be to grow in holiness — not to be "perfectionists," where we lose sight of the ultimate goal: to become like Christ; to be perfect, not for perfection's sake, but out of love for God and those around us.

Love is the primary motivator of the human will. If we can focus on what we love, we will find ourselves very motivated. If you are a melancholic, you should remind yourself to focus your attention on the most *important* goals and allow other things to slide; in other words, don't sweat the small stuff. If you fail to prioritize carefully, you may exhaust yourself — physically or mentally — and annoy those around you by attending to every minor detail. When we forget that God is first, our spouse second, and our children third, we might inadvertently put our kids or our spouse on a level above God, and over-attend to every detail of their lives, which can be smothering indeed!

Once the melancholic has his goals prioritized, however, he might need a kick-start. The melancholic temperament favors the intellect, which always prefers analysis to action. Hence, the melancholic is not *ready* to respond now, but is rather slow and pensive. It can be difficult for him to begin a project. He feels it necessary to ponder each aspect of the situation from all angles and reconsider everything before he can make a judgment or take action.

> **MELANCHOLIC**
>
> **Motivational strengths**: High ideals and commitment to perfection. Analyzes projects thoroughly.
>
> **Weaknesses:** Sometimes needs a "kick-start." Can be critical or skeptical about new jobs, approaches, or models.
>
> **Challenges:** Needs to build confidence in order not to globalize anxiety or negativity. Must learn not to procrastinate or obsess about details.

If you are working with a melancholic, you may have noticed that he balks when asked to work on a big project. He may verbally express all the reasons the project will not succeed. At best, he is markedly unenthusiastic. His preference will be to analyze the situation in greater depth. If you begin to push him too hard toward action, he can become overwhelmed.

His analytic tendency to uncover all potential problems and obstacles can further inhibit action. He envisions all the potential disasters and thinks to himself, "This can never be done," or "This project is doomed," or some other gloomy thought. Not only will he face all potential obstacles, worst-case scenarios, and disasters possible for the project, but he will begin to envision all future projects to be accomplished by close friends and family members (as well as the depressing state of world politics and the cultural climate of licentiousness). Thus the web of disaster and despair spreads. Such "globalizing anxiety" can have a stultifying effect upon the melancholic. Sometimes, as a result, the melancholic will simply withdraw, paralyzed, and take no action whatsoever.

Once you have prioritized the goals, remind the melancholic of two things: first, that you are asking him to do only this *one* small task; you are not asking him to balance the national budget or to end poverty in America. Second, he is the right — no, the *perfect* — person for this task. His talents and skills are absolutely vital for the success of this project. To motivate the melancholic, you need to simplify the target and reassure him that he is able to do it.

Our oldest daughter was a classic melancholic in this regard, especially in her younger years. In high school, when big tests were imminent, or a huge project was due, her globalized anxiety would be felt throughout the house. It seemed that the more she despaired, the longer it took her to get started, and someone

would usually have to "talk her down."
Sometimes, we would even have to
help kick-start her with a particularly
daunting prospect (finding a job, for
example). But, once she got started, she
would roll ahead unswerving, toward a
perfect A or toward becoming a model
employee.

If you are a melancholic and have
set your sights high, but find yourself
becoming overwhelmed by negativity or
obstacles, stop to reflect that you must
take only one small step at a time, and
envision how you can accomplish that
step. Try not to worry about the future:
seventy percent of all such worries are about events that will never
occur anyway.

If you are trying to motivate a melancholic spouse or child, you
will be tempted to minimalize his worries or attempt to cheer him
up. This may not help. He might think you don't understand the
issues or his feelings or will increase the level of anxiety in an attempt to convince you of the seriousness of the issue. The best way
to help him out of the global-anxiety mode is to be empathic with
him, to let him know that you understand how he sees the situation and the seriousness of the problem. Once you have shown
empathy, you can ask him to envision just one small part of the
program and encourage him to get started on just that one detail
or that first step.

Another trap to avoid is to try to solve his problems. The melancholic does not want to be told, "This is how you should do it,"
because that only reinforces his feeling of helplessness or inability

to solve the problem. Offer to help, but not to take over for him. (In fact, nobody really wants that; it infringes on our free will.) To build confidence, you might try brainstorming possible solutions, reminding the melancholic of his past successes, and eliciting willingness to just take the first step. Always encourage supernatural optimism and true confidence — which can come only from confidence in God. Lead him to reflect on the great blessings in his life: gifts from God.

∽

Key points for the melancholic

• *Is this really important?* Before the melancholic begins to list a hundred obstacles to the problem or issue at hand, ask him to examine the worthiness of the project. In the larger scheme of things, is this really important?

• *What a blessing!* Encourage the virtue of optimism (which combats downheartedness and depression). Only confidence in God gives us *true* confidence in ourselves. Develop trust in God. Reflect verbally on the great blessings in your life: gifts from God. When helping a melancholic child, remind him that you (the parent) are willing to help out if necessary. Help him learn how to make the *best* of each situation.

• *Acknowledge the obstacles.* The melancholic will be already coming up with forty-seven reasons the task is doomed to failure. If you don't acknowledge the obstacles *yourself*, you are contributing to the melancholic's feeling that, if they don't bring up the problems, nobody will! Although the task is formidable, you have confidence that they can do it!

♦ *What is the worst that could happen?* Whether you or a loved one is experiencing anxiety or fear about taking a new step or starting a daunting project, ask the question: *What is your worst fear?* This sometimes helps us to realize that the worst thing that could happen may not be that bad! And this breaks through the barrier of inaction or indecision.

♦ *Be strong!* Develop fortitude. The melancholic needs to develop this great virtue to combat fear, self-pity, and sadness. As a parent, you can help your children overcome their fears by breaking them down into manageable portions and conquering them one at a time. Fortitude means that we accept even the worst situations with a sportsman-like attitude.

How to Motivate Yourself and Others

MOTIVATING THE SANGUINE
The challenge: Persevering until the end

Sanguines are lively and eager right out of the gate. They are enthusiastic, full of ideas, and are avid to begin. In fact, they will be eager to start on *many* projects! But some races are sprints, and others are marathons. The sanguine needs help with the long runs. Because impressions are not lasting, they are quickly followed by new impressions. As a result, the sanguine appears to be volatile and changeable in his moods or whims, and tends to be weak in follow-through.

With his lively interest in people and his good social skills, the sanguine will also be more than willing to help out on others' projects. He will also eagerly enlist *your* aid in working on *his* projects. He is a natural salesman, and, with his great facility for speech, he may sell you on an idea that he is not committed to himself! The sanguine is optimistic and tends to overlook difficulties. As a result, he may not carefully consider truly significant obstacles when developing a plan. How often has a parent heard from a sanguine child, "Oh, that test will be a piece of cake!"

If you are a sanguine, you are naturally friendly, relationships are important to you, and you will tend to agree with your friends. Thus, you may have to be careful not to jump to conclusions, let your decisions be influenced by what other people like or want, or be taken in by unscrupulous individuals. Your optimistic temperament may not see all the potential obstacles or difficulties involved in a particular course of action, so you may imprudently make an unwise choice.

If you work with a sanguine, you might find that, while he is highly creative, inspirational, and can easily engender enthusiasm for a new project, his tendency to overconfidence, insufficient reflection about significant details, or lack of commitment can result in an unfinished project or one that lands on others' shoulders.

Our thirteen-year-old exhibits classic sanguine self-confidence: he is sure that all the girls like him, that he is the funniest kid in class, and that he will get straight As on his report card. When he takes a big test, he comes home confidently predicting an A. Then he gets the test back, and it's a B minus — every time. "I don't understand it!" he wails. "I was *sure* I got them all right!" Nonetheless, by the time the next test rolls around, he has forgotten this setback and predicts another A. We have to help him connect the dots between hard work and good study habits and the A he really wants to achieve.

Sanguines face their greatest challenge in making prudential (rather than impulsive) decisions, in their attention to detail, and in their follow-through. Like long-distance runners, sanguines must *slow down* to keep going. Are they looking at all the important details? Have they considered all the obstacles? Have they thought things through, or are they merely hoping all will go well? Still, because of their optimism, insight, and good cheer, they will be a welcome addition to any team. If they fail, they will pick themselves right up and start anew.

SANGUINE

Motivational strengths: Creative, enthusiastic, inspiring team player. Easy to get "fired up," at least initially.

Weaknesses: May overlook details or be overly confident. May agree with others rather than take an unpopular position. Can become easily discouraged by grinding details or obstacles.

Challenges: Needs help in setting up a schedule and following through. May give up if the job loses its fun, so needs good structure and positive direction.

∞

Key points for the sanguine

• *Hard work + patience = rewards.* Remind your sanguine that hard work pays off. Tie his work directly to a reward that he really wants. Make sure he is rewarded along the way, to help him persevere until the end. Eventually, he will develop the habit. Acknowledge successes, and point out how hard work and perseverance contributed to the success.

• *Can you study this in more depth?* Walk your sanguine through the process of studying or accomplishing a task in depth and with attention to detail. He wants to be finished in a hurry and to accomplish the task with a sweeping brush stroke. *Show* him what it is like to notice the details. While he is young, develop his powers of observation by playing memory games or asking him to recount exactly what happened in a show; later, develop *discernment* by questioning the validity of arguments he hears on the news or reads in the paper. What is fact? What is opinion?

> **MOTIVATING COMMENTS FOR THE SANGUINE**
>
> "Very exciting!"
>
> "I love your ideas!"
>
> "Let's work on this together!"
>
> "Let's go to Starbucks and write up a proposal, make a time line, and set up a schedule."

• *Can I help you set up a schedule?* Help the sanguine plan interim goals (to keep him on task) with interim rewards, and set up a schedule. Reflect on the positive outcomes he will achieve through discipline and planning. Buy a planner, and review it weekly.

MOTIVATING THE PHLEGMATIC
The challenge: Overcoming obstacles

Phlegmatics, because of their cooperative, quiet nature, are beloved by many, but they have often been accused of laziness, unassertiveness, or a lack of leadership ability or initiative. In fact, phlegmatics can be great leaders, with their ability to remain calm under pressure, their iron strength of will, and their mediating ability; it is all a matter of correct motivation.

No one would guess our pastor is a phlegmatic. He is a spiritual leader of the parish, a role model for his parishioners, and truly "another Christ." He is also a creative organizer and leads the diocese in raising funds for our building campaign. He knows everyone's name in his parish of nearly a thousand families! He has more than a hundred audiotapes of talks he has given on spiritual and human formation — including marriage and family issues, personal development, and apologetics.[39] He is an unparalleled leader.

But this is an instance of someone who knows and understands his temperament and leads with his best qualities. He has taken the time to learn how to motivate others, how to encourage leadership, how to make everyone feel welcome and a significant part of the team, and how to draw out the best in each one. He also knows when to take a much-needed break.

If you are a phlegmatic, your two biggest challenges will be in setting goals and in overcoming obstacles. Because you place a high priority on harmonious relationships and cooperation, you will be tempted to conform to the expectations and goals of those

---

[39] Available on the website of Father Francis Peffley at www.transporter.com.

around you. Thus, your goals may be lower than they ought to be, based on the level of the bar of those with whom you associate, your fellow students, your family members, and so forth.

Secondly, you tend to be other-centered and aim to please. But obstacles and the unknown future can be frightening rather than motivating. You tend to respond to what is happening in the moment and have some trepidation about looking into the future.

Furthermore, when faced with what appear to be insurmountable obstacles, or with potential humiliation, scorn, or contempt, you may be tempted to shy away from the task. When confronted by belittling or nagging or overly punitive threats, you tend to withdraw and retreat into yourself. If your family of origin was particularly punitive or belittling, you might have developed a habit of underachievement.

If you are working with a phlegmatic, you may be tempted to try to set goals for him or to take over for him on a project. Unlike other temperaments, who will react negatively to such an attempt, the phlegmatic may let you do it! It is nonetheless a mistake. Over time, it will erode his self-confidence and make him less likely to learn to take charge.

> **PHLEGMATIC**
>
> **Motivational strengths:**
> Calm in crises, naturally cooperative. Open to help and advice.
>
> **Weaknesses:** Often tempted to take the road of least resistance. Easily discouraged.
>
> **Challenges:** Needs to see the big picture and be motivated to set big goals. Needs to be greatly encouraged and positively held accountable at all stages of the process.

Phlegmatics react best to confidence-building motivation. It is completely *unhelpful* to dwell on their failures or mistakes; this only discourages them and causes them to withdraw. So often,

> **MOTIVATING COMMENTS FOR THE PHLEGMATIC**
>
> "You're a key player in this project."
>
> "I am so impressed with your work in this area."
>
> "Let's talk about some ideas you might have for the future."
>
> "Let's set some time lines to measure your progress."

people are tempted to nag or push the phlegmatic, when it seems as if he does not grasp the urgency of a situation. This is an understandable attempt to help the adaptable phlegmatic to understand the importance of change. But it is likely to backfire, by creating too great a discrepancy between where we are and where we want to be. The phlegmatic will feel overwhelmed or incapable. The task will become formidable and the obstacles insurmountable. Thus, a delicate balance must be struck between creating a sense of urgency and importance and building up the phlegmatic's confidence to achieve it.

∞

Key points for the phlegmatic

• *Ask evocative questions:* "I can really see you achieving this important goal. What might be your first step?" Or "I know you can accomplish this. How might you go about making this change?" Or "What obstacles do you foresee?"

• *Use a confidence ruler:* "On a scale of zero to ten, with zero being not at all confident and ten being extremely confident, where would you say you are? How could you get to a higher number?"

• *Review past successes:* "Remember the time you thought you couldn't get an A in that class, but you did? How did you do that?" But even when something was not a success: "You gave it a great effort! Let's talk about what you might have done differently."

• *Acknowledge personal strengths*: "What's so great about you is that you are such a calm person under pressure!" or "Everyone respects you for your fairness!"

• *Instill accountability* to track progress and retain focus on the goal.

Chapter 9

∞

Discovering Your Secondary Temperament

"He is as valiant as the lion, churlish
as the bear, slow as the elephant: a man
into whom nature hath so crowded humors
that his valor is crushed into folly, his folly
sauced with discretion. . . . He is melancholy
without cause and merry against the hair."

Troilus and Cressida

"But God is to be worshiped;
all men are not alike."

As You Like It

∞

As you read about the four basic temperaments, you will likely discover that while one of the types most accurately describes your personality, a few characteristics might not apply; instead, a significant number of the characteristics of another temperament apply. These characteristics typically come from our *secondary temperament*. Most people, in fact, are not purely of one temperament but a combination of two, a primary one and a secondary one.

This is generally a good thing. Conrad Hock asserts in *The Four Temperaments* that in general "a person is happier if his temperament is not a pure one."[40] Temperament combinations help balance the strengths and weaknesses of our personalities. And in times of stress, the characteristics of our secondary temperament can be useful in handling situations where we've deemed (consciously or subconsciously) our primary temperament inadequate.

∞

Impossible combinations?

Some authors have proposed that an individual may have three or four temperaments, or that the temperaments can be combined so that two diametrically opposed temperaments are combined in one individual (such as the choleric-phlegmatic combination or the melancholic-sanguine combination).[41]

[40]Hock, *The Four Temperaments*, 48.
[41]Tim LaHaye, *Why You Act the Way You Do* (Wheaton, Illinois: Living Books, 1984), 37 ff.

We maintain that this is not accurate. Although we believe that two temperaments can be (and most often are) combined, there is a limit to the combinations possible. Remember that, classified according to patterns of reaction, the temperaments are distinguished according to whether the reaction to stimuli is quick or delayed, intense or dull, sustained over time or not sustained. We have all encountered individuals who react quickly and intensely for the most part, but on some occasions may have a delayed, although intense, reaction. And we all know someone who, although for the most part a very laid-back, easy-going individual, can have an intense, although short-lived outburst in certain situations. And, as mentioned in an earlier chapter, the very saintly individual may have so conquered his passions and natural inclinations (especially those that are less desirable) that his natural temperament is not easily discernible to others.

But it becomes difficult, if not impossible, to imagine a mentally healthy individual whose natural reactions, throughout his life, are quick, intense, and sustained, yet at the same time slow, dull, and unsustained. Can an individual be naturally both introverted and extraverted? Can his reactions be both intense and dull?

Therefore, the two combinations that are, by nature, untenable in a healthy individual are, we believe, the choleric-phlegmatic and the sanguine-melancholic combinations.[42] Such individuals

___

[42]Florence Littauer, author of *Personality Plus* and numerous other books on the temperaments, maintains that these "split personalities" can lead to "emotional problems," and are the result of *learned* behaviors, often in response to a dysfunctional upbringing, which mask the true personality (Florence Littauer, *Personality Plus* [Grand Rapids: Fleming H. Revell, 2001], 146). If indeed this is a "mask of survival," as Littauer suggests, or learned, rather

would have to be at once introverted and extraverted; slow, yet quick, to respond; intense, yet dull in their responses; and their responses would last a long time and yet a short time.[43] In every way and in every aspect of themselves, they would be internally conflicted.

At first glance, you might assume that a phlegmatic who otherwise exhibits strong leadership skills is highly competitive, or is very driven in terms of his chosen field, is a choleric-phlegmatic. However, we have never met anyone with an in-depth knowledge of the temperaments who claims to be this combination. Such a person would be both driven and laid-back, argumentative and yet non-confrontational. He would relish conflict and lean into controversy at the same time as being a gentle peacemaker, avoiding conflict!

We have, however, met phlegmatics who are remarkable leaders who accomplish many things. We know some very competitive phlegmatics. But they do not attribute their success to a hefty dose of choler. Rather, these individuals have taken the strength of will of their phlegmatic temperament and used it to develop their own leadership capacity — usually at the service of Christ! Our pastor is one such example.

Our son is an example of a competitive phlegmatic. Because he has always been highly competitive and involved in many sports,

than God-given, our position remains upheld; namely, that the fundamental, God-given temperament is not an inherently self-contradictory one.

[43]Tim LaHaye, author of *Why You Act the Way You Do*, maintains that there are twelve temperament blends. Although otherwise a very interesting book, we think this concept of twelve blends is due to a lack of understanding of the underlying causes of the differences in temperament, based on patterns of reaction.

we did not at first realize that he was phlegmatic. One day, after quietly listening to a conversation about temperaments, he just calmly inserted, "I'm a phlegmatic!" We were at first surprised, but then realized how accurately the phlegmatic temperament described our son's personality: his quiet cooperation and peaceful nature — except during card games or when on a sports team, when he exhibited a steely determination to win. We surmised that, within the environment of repeated success in sports and lots of positive encouragement, he has become a very "active" phlegmatic — with many trophies and awards to his name. Yet, if he had sensed that he couldn't possibly have won or had never been encouraged to try a sport, his phlegmatic temperament would have taken over, and he wouldn't even have made an effort.

Another example is gold-medalist swimmer Ian Crocker. A friend of his once commented, "If you were any more laid-back, you'd be dead." But no one becomes an Olympic gold medalist and a world-record holder without intense (although perhaps hidden) drive.

We have met a few people who, when they first hear of the temperaments, believe they are sanguine-melancholic (or melancholic-sanguine). They tend to be extraverted worriers who have fabulous people skills, but lack decisiveness. They are warm and friendly and able to relate to other people quickly, yet they lack follow-through and can be severely disorganized procrastinators. They rightly identify themselves as partly sanguine, because they have the people skills, the creativity, the warmth, and the optimism of the sanguine. Yet they believe they must also be melancholic because they tend to worry — a lot. They worry about conversations they recently had, how they ought to have responded, what is the correct action to take in a particular situation, and whether other people are judging them harshly. They can be extremely indecisive, and this results in procrastination and disorganization. They may have a *longing for the ideal* that leads them to believe they have perfectionist tendencies.

However, a sanguine-melancholic combination would be someone who is not only extraverted, optimistic, quick to respond, scattered, and forgiving, but also introverted, pessimistic, slow to respond, meticulous, and unforgiving. Such conflict in a mentally healthy individual is impossible to conceive.

These happy, extraverted, but somewhat unfocused sanguines have come to believe (through peer influence, faith conversion, study, or a mentor) that their natural temperament is lacking in depth; they believe they *ought* to be deep, introspective thinkers, orderly and perfect in all their undertakings. Their natural confident optimism has become clouded by self-doubt and hesitation. Self-doubt and self-chastisement lead them to conclude that they are melancholic. In fact, they are still impulsive and somewhat disorganized — sanguine — but now self-consciously and unhappily so. Their lack of self-knowledge reveals the sanguine temperament's tendency to superficiality, while their sensitivity and desire to please others makes them want to be "perfect" for their spouse, friends, or a teacher.

When these sanguine types make a cursory study of the temperaments, they observe in themselves a certain indecisiveness, and they mistakenly attribute this to melancholic "introspection." Yet the melancholic's indecisiveness comes not so much from self-doubt as from an overabundance of reflection. When the sanguine exhibits indecisiveness, on the other hand, it is *not* the result of much reflection and introspection. It is typically the opposite. The sanguine will not take the time to reflect deeply on the issue and has instead frittered away his time consulting others (in his extraverted fashion). The indecisiveness of the sanguine stems typically from a lack of self-discipline, then, rather than the melancholic's over-reflection and irresoluteness. In the sanguine's indecisiveness you will sense a fundamental optimism; a sanguine will often relate a funny anecdote about his own indecisiveness. The melancholic, on the other hand, might exhibit what appears to be indecisiveness, but is rather an inability to act, for fear of the consequences or else due to his overly analytical nature. (Hamlet was a classic melancholic.) If you are unsure whether you are sanguine or melancholic, ask yourself whether you are primarily extraverted or introverted, whether you are quick to respond or slow to respond, and whether you are fundamentally optimistic or pessimistic.

Apart from these, all other temperament combinations are possible, and are seen to one degree or another in most people. Let's look at them now.

SANGUINE-CHOLERIC AND CHOLERIC-SANGUINE

The sanguine-choleric is the most extraverted of all the temperament combinations. The good news is that, with this combination, the optimistic, impulsive, fun-loving sanguine becomes more capable of follow-through, taking significant leadership roles, and juggling many projects without unduly sacrificing productivity. This temperament tends to be a happy combination of decisiveness and charm, analytical skills and creativity, friendliness with reliability.

Your ability to connect with people should tone down some of the "bulldozer" characteristics of the pure choleric. You are insightful and enthusiastic, with good people skills. You are also capable of constancy, dedication, and serious undertakings, although at times you may be underestimated, due to your often humorous and lighthearted manner. You not only are capable of creative inspirations, but also you will find within yourself the persistence and drive needed to carry out your inspirations.

St. Peter may have been a sanguine-choleric. He was impulsive, enthusiastic, protective, talkative, frequently wrong — yet a heroic and passionate leader of the flock.

The bad news is that, if intellectual, human, or spiritual formation is seriously lacking, this temperament blend can exhibit the *worst* of the two temperaments: overly talkative, brassy, opinionated, loud, rash, swift to jump to conclusions, and forgetful. If intellectual depth is lacking, this temperament mixture can become brash, bossy, and intolerant. The high-spirited humor of the sanguine can become biting and hurtful when combined with the unforgiving, vengeful nature of the poorly formed choleric. If pleasure-seeking and impulsivity are not contained, the sanguine-choleric may wind up with a lax conscience that justifies his weaknesses, ultimately resulting in habitual sin. On the other hand, the natural generosity flowing from the sanguine temperament will commit him to many good works.

If you are a sanguine-choleric, because you are easily inspired at the outset, you may find that you are very actively involved in many projects. But take care that you do not let the sanguine side take over to the extent that you are "all talk and no action." Many sanguine-cholerics have to watch out for a tendency to come up with great ideas, put everyone to work, and then drop the ball when the project gets tiresome.

The choleric-sanguine will be somewhat less extraverted than the sanguine-choleric, because the choleric's extraversion often takes a backseat to his goal-oriented behavior. Thus, this temperament mix will result in a highly driven leader (choleric) whose social skills and interest in other people (sanguine) make him less dictatorial. He will be more compassionate in dealing with people, less controlling than the pure choleric, more flexible, and more willing to take time out to relax and enjoy himself (and other people).

If you are a choleric-sanguine, you will find that you have a great amount of energy and inspiration for initiating projects and can be highly focused on task completion as well. Although you tend to be very objective, pragmatic, and logical — and may sometimes find yourself stepping on toes in the process of accomplishing the task at hand — you will also have the interpersonal skills needed to resolve conflict and to help people work together and get along with one another. The creativity and sensitivity of your sanguine nature will enable you to be flexible when the situation calls for it, and less demanding and harsh than a pure choleric would tend to be.

Without strong formation and a deep spiritual life, however, your temperament's weaknesses will be intensified. Without attention to self-formation you may find yourself quickly aroused to anger, yet also unforgiving. You can be impatient with others and speak frankly or impulsively without regard for others' feelings. You may become a workaholic or driven by your passions. You may insist on having your own way, and become angered, blame others, or make excuses when corrected. But, once you become aware of the weaknesses of your nature, and make a commitment to self-improvement, you will be able to be equally determined in pursuing self-formation.

St. Teresa of Avila, mystic and Doctor of the Church, may have been of choleric-sanguine temperament. As a child, St. Teresa was impulsive and headstrong. After reading about the Crusades, she packed her bags and ran away from home — dragging her brother Rodrigo with her — in the hope that together they would die a martyr's death at the hands of the Moors!

She loved to read the sixteenth-century equivalent of romance novels; she would hide the frivolous volumes under her bed. She was a bit vain and, as a young teen, loved to fix her hair, dress in the latest fashion, wear perfume and cosmetics, and gossip with her friends. Yet her sanguine loquaciousness was tempered by choleric intelligence and drive; once she became committed to following Christ, she ran away from home (for the second time!) and joined the Carmelites. Yet she did not settle for a halfhearted convent life — one that, she felt, had departed from the original spirit of the founder — but resolved to found her own convent, which became the reformed, discalced Carmelites.

"Teresa had beauty, charm, literary genius . . . an administrative ability second to none; humor and tenderness and common sense; the resourcefulness of a great soldier. . . ."[44] Doesn't this sound like the best qualities of the choleric and sanguine temperaments?

CHOLERIC-MELANCHOLIC AND MELANCHOLIC-CHOLERIC

The choleric-melancholic mixture combines two passionate and persevering temperaments to create a strong leader with the ability to envision a great plan of action — someone who is both meticulous and strategic. The tendency of the choleric to make hasty, often sweeping judgments will be tempered by the melancholic's careful analysis and reflection. The tendency of the melancholic to be moody, hypercritical, and slow to act will be counterbalanced by the optimism and practicality of the choleric. Thus, the choleric-melancholic will be capable of decisive — yet thoughtful — action and will be thoroughly productive.

[44] William Thomas Walsh, *Saint Teresa of Avila: A Biography* (Rockford, Illinois: TAN Books, 1943, 1987), 1.

If you are a choleric-melancholic, you have a quick, analytical mind, possibly with great attention to detail, with a strong sense of order and discipline. You will be more extraverted than a pure melancholic or a melancholic-choleric, and you will be able to take on more projects and accomplish more things than a pure melancholic would be capable of. We know several choleric-melancholics (and melancholic-cholerics) who are CFOs; their leadership ability, combined with their meticulous attention to financial detail, makes them valued in this sphere. (In addition to their analytical skills and attention to detail, they tend also to be highly ethical, honest employees.)

You will most likely have a strong analytical mind, holding other people and institutions to high standards. As a parent, you might be the strongest disciplinarian of all the temperaments: setting high standards for your children, while being somewhat difficult to please, prone to anger and unforgiveness, and tempted to punish harshly. (Both of these temperaments tend to unforgiveness, so this will be an area in which spiritual growth will be a challenge.)

Self-sacrificing, yet driven, the choleric-melancholic can accomplish great things. Without human and spiritual formation, however, this combination can result in an individual who is proud and obstinate, with deep anger and resentment. He can be opinionated, critical, and judgmental. A quick intelligence, the tendency to think he is always right, and his pursuit of the ideal might make someone with this temperament combination autocratic, moody, arrogant, and antisocial.

We imagine that St. Paul was choleric-melancholic; he was intense, focused, and driven. He was not one to value relationships above rules. He disagreed with St. Peter on several occasions (as he wrote to the Galatians: "And when Cephas came to Antioch, I opposed him to his face because he clearly was wrong" [Gal. 2:11]) and even parted ways from his fellow missionary Barnabus, because Barnabus wanted to bring along John Mark, whom Paul said had deserted them at Pamphylia (Acts 15:37-39). The melancholic-choleric is also a leader with the potential to accomplish great works. However, whereas the choleric-melancholic is driven by the challenge and the opportunity, the melancholic-choleric is inspired more by the nobility of the task. The melancholic side of both temperament combinations results in the project's being organized and significant, while the choleric aspect is the driving and demanding force.

If you are melancholic-choleric, you are somewhat less pragmatic (or utilitarian) than a pure choleric, just as persevering and determined, and with a greater emphasis on high and noble ideals. Likely to be motivated by the most noble and demanding of causes, you are capable of founding a humanitarian society, composing a symphony, founding a school, or discovering a cure. You are organized, perfectionist, introspective, driven, and moody (although less so than a pure melancholic). You will be less active than a choleric-melancholic and less extraverted, more internally focused.

But your weaknesses include a tendency to excessive self-criticism and criticism of others, being dismissive or overly judgmental, exhibiting self-absorption and a lack of trust, and possessing a controlling nature. You tend to be inflexible, can bear grudges for a long time, and may be prone to discouragement. A melancholic-choleric who is not attentive to his spiritual life and does not keep his eye assiduously on the truly important things of life can become a cross to those around him, through his nit-picking, perfectionism, disdain, resentfulness, spitefulness when crossed, and even haughtiness.

PHLEGMATIC-MELANCHOLIC
AND MELANCHOLIC-PHLEGMATIC

The phlegmatic-melancholic is definitively introverted; thus, anxieties or deep emotions may not be clearly expressed. Those with this combination will react most slowly of all the temperaments. They may appear — or believe themselves — at times to be lazy. As a result of his delayed and sometimes dull response, a phlegmatic-melancholic will be slower to speak out, tempted to procrastinate, and reticent. At times when the melancholic aspect dominates, he will have plenty of time to mull over in his mind what his response *should have* been. He may become easily offended or discouraged. The phlegmatic attentiveness to relationships, and to getting along and keeping the peace, will take the edge off some of the melancholic tendency to perfectionism and critical judgments of others. On the other hand, because he may be more easily offended, he might want to express criticism of others yet hesitant to confront directly. The dominance of the phlegmatic temperament may also drive the melancholic proclivity to order and neatness out of the picture.

If you are a phlegmatic-melancholic, you will show a cooperative spirit and a desire to please, and will value harmonious relationships. You are particularly gifted in teaching, mediating among groups, and counseling individuals. And although yours isn't the most dynamic temperament, your lack of defensiveness, your calmness under pressure, and your gift for mediation in critical situations can make you a very effective servant-leader, one who is willing to roll up his sleeves and work along with those he leads by example.

This temperament combination can face at times a greater challenge to your confidence than other temperaments (especially the choleric or sanguine). For this reason, when you are facing a major challenge or have been given a multifaceted and demanding project, it will be absolutely critical for you to maintain your level of energy and motivation — not to mention your prayer life — to complete the project. You will want to anticipate the way your moods can get you off track and take concrete steps to maintain accountability in order to remain focused and energized throughout the task. Motivational tapes, exercise, a healthy diet, spiritual guidance, and a strong sacramental life will be critical. You will also need to maintain your focus on the big picture at all times and not be distracted by the "urgent" demands of the moment, or by what other people may ask of you. To this end, it is always wise to seek regular professional, personal, and spiritual guidance from qualified individuals. In order for the phlegmatic temperament to achieve success and reach his goals, he should always work with a motivational program that provides structure, inspires confidence, and ensures accountability.

The melancholic-phlegmatic is tidier and more procedural than the phlegmatic-melancholic. He may be slower to take on new projects, as the melancholic fear of new situations and the tendency to perfectionism take over. The double-dose of introversion, along with the melancholic tendency to negativity, makes it difficult for him to give compliments and make upbeat small talk. It also causes him instinctively to say no when he first hears a request. Others may perceive this as snobbishness. Unless the melancholic-phlegmatic is very comfortable, and is surrounded by understanding, long-time friends, he may find himself somewhat isolated and alone, unable to warm up in a social gathering.

One melancholic-phlegmatic we know is highly organized, critical, slow, and dogmatically unforgiving, yet reveals her phlegmatic aspect in her intense discomfort with confrontation (unless she is *very* at ease among the warring members) and in her strong relationships with her friends. You wouldn't guess that she is so devoted to her friends, however, because, true to her melancholic nature, she rarely initiates contact with them; they always have to call her first.

If you are phlegmatic-melancholic, it's likely that you are a bit more upbeat than the melancholic-phlegmatic, a little less introverted, more trusting, slightly less moody, more generous with your time, and a more gracious host. You will rarely find yourself angry (although your feelings may be easily hurt), forgive more readily, and do not hold on to hurts in the same way that a more dominantly melancholic temperament would. You are compassionate, sensitive, caring, and tend to gravitate toward the helping professions. You are a patient and caring teacher. You are not as perfectionist as a pure melancholic, and you generally struggle with organization. You find it difficult to set limits or turn someone down who asks a favor of you; you may be especially drawn to volunteer or missionary work, the apostolate, or other works of mercy. Although very generous, you may find it difficult to set priorities or limits. Your phlegmatic side makes it hard to say no. Sometimes your generosity can result in not enough time to get organized, to be prepared, or to relax. Burn-out and feeling overwhelmed may result.

Relaxation is something you really do enjoy and need, though. You need time to unwind, to be alone, and to recuperate from the stress of hard work or demanding interactions. You may have a tendency to procrastinate, which results in becoming swamped and overwhelmed, requiring days to recuperate from the stress, leading to procrastination . . . and the cycle begins again.

Although your weak link may be organizational and procedural planning, and you can sometimes be a bit too thin-skinned, you are a key member of any team. You are very adaptable and flexible, are able to succeed in start-ups and unstructured settings, and are able to work with a wide range of temperaments and personalities, due to your strong relationship and mediatory skills. With supportive supervision and disciplined accountability, you will be able to reach ambitious long-term goals.

SANGUINE-PHLEGMATIC
AND PHLEGMATIC-SANGUINE

The sanguine-phlegmatic is an extraverted, optimistic, warm individual who readily connects with others and is well liked by all. His sanguine side makes him creative, enthusiastic, friendly, and inspiring. His phlegmatic side makes him somewhat cautious at times, and also highly sensitive to other people's moods, emotions, likes, and dislikes. He keenly desires harmony in relationships.

He tends to overextend himself to meet others' needs and to personalize any negative criticism. (If the boss says, "We are not meeting our quotas," the sanguine-phlegmatic thinks, "Is he angry at me?" If her best friend says, "I really can't wear red lipstick," the sanguine-phlegmatic will think, "She's trying to tell me that *my* lipstick looks terrible!") After all, the sanguine-phlegmatic has a double-dose of *feeling;* twice blessed by the tendency to prioritize relationships and harmony.

If you are a sanguine-phlegmatic, most everyone likes you! You are easy-going, creative, fun-loving, enthusiastic, imaginative, caring, generous, flexible, and spontaneous. You may be considered "emotional" because of your easily aroused feelings, your attentiveness to relationships, and your tender heart. Your weaknesses are superficiality, indecisiveness, disorganization, and procrastination. Often you find it difficult to know exactly how to state what you mean, or how to express yourself logically; this contributes to a tendency to talk more than is needed or to provide more detail than is necessary. (You might find your more logical spouse's eyes glazing over as you tell a story, or might find that he inserts words for you.)

You can be easily influenced (which is exacerbated by your tendency to ask others for advice — without thinking it through) and to do what seems kind before considering whether it is objectively right. Many sanguine-phlegmatics are drawn to teaching (and parenting), the helping professions, and volunteer works for the Church or for the welfare of society. You place a high priority on your personal search for meaning and self-identity. The strong need to discover your "true self" will be met by a rich prayer life and a personal relationship with Christ.

Your weaknesses probably tend to bother you more than anyone else. For example, you may find yourself blurting out something without thinking, or spending too much time seeking advice, only to find yourself more confused than when you started, or oversleeping every day this week — despite all the best intentions. You may find yourself becoming overcommitted because you simply can't say no and have a strong need to be liked and to please people.

A typical sanguine-phlegmatic trick is to spend too much money shopping or (better yet) dining out with friends, and then to put off balancing the checkbook (too much work, too many other distractions) until it is hopelessly behind. Now you are overwhelmed with everything that has piled up! You may complain halfheartedly, blame circumstances, or go shopping, but you may not really make a concerted effort to change.

If you are a phlegmatic-sanguine, however, your phlegmatic side will dominate. This will result in a greater tendency to introversion (although still less than a melancholic's or pure phlegmatic's). You are peace-loving, conservative, well-balanced, easy-going, with a dry wit and a talent for bringing people together. As an employee, you are compliant, dutiful, orderly, and subdued (and probably were as a child, too). Others may not realize that you have a sanguine side — at first. It may take a little longer for you to make close friends,[45] but once you do, your sanguine nature can assert itself. It will also show up when, for example, you have been so dutiful and compliant about work or school that finally you need to relax and unwind — and now the sanguine, fun-loving side comes out. Or, when you are hanging out with your closest friends.

You are very thoughtful of others, with a knack for empathically putting yourself in other people's shoes, and you value peace and harmony at all times. You also have a great sense of humor and an easy-going manner that makes you a valued friend. You are discouraged by criticism and negativity and need acceptance, support, and cooperation in your personal life. You can be deeply wounded by sarcasm, harsh criticism, and anger when it is directed at you. You will not, however, directly fight back, but prefer to turn the other cheek or redouble your efforts to please.

Phlegmatic-sanguines tend to prefer movies, concerts, or other forms of relaxation that are a bit more spectator-oriented. When they attend parties, they tend to prefer smaller groups, rather than the large social gatherings a pure sanguine enjoys. Like sanguine-phlegmatics, they are very attentive to relationships, to harmony among people. They have deep feelings, hate negative criticism, and become discouraged by negativity in those around them. They are strongly tempted to repress their own wishes in order to preserve peace in a relationship. A stressful situation (especially

---

[45] In fact, friendships are very important for this temperament. If there are no friends, this could lead to an unhealthy, solitary lifestyle (television, videogames) and even depression.

one that is interpersonally demanding) may cause the peaceful phlegmatic-sanguine to withdraw into solitary television watching, playing computer games, eating, or sleeping, instead of directly expressing his negative feelings.

A danger for the phlegmatic-sanguine is to be satisfied with achieving less than what he is capable of — whether because he tends not to plan for the future or because the more challenging goals seem to be too much trouble. A phlegmatic-sanguine will be strongly tempted to quit if he doesn't think the end product is worth the effort or if he fears he won't succeed.

As a friend, the phlegmatic-sanguine is true-blue. He is likely to be a great listener and can help others solve their problems. He is a calm and objective mediator — so long as he is not himself personally entwined in the conflict. Attention to self-formation through goal-setting, thinking about the future, and seeking expert advice will help the phlegmatic-sanguine become productive, successful, and a great leader.

Perhaps the most besetting difficulties for this temperament combination are the natural inclination to peace and quiet (tempting you to laziness), a preference to live within the moment (superficiality), and a tendency to make decisions based first on the desire to please someone else or to restore harmony. You are a supportive friend and a cooperative employee; but at times, this can cause you to say yes to the demands of friends or colleagues without first analyzing whether this choice is actually the best one to make. At times, wanting to either please your good friends or to avoid conflict at home or at work, you may go with the flow when in fact a strong stance is necessary. Or, you may avoid a more demanding task or career move in order to maintain harmony and stability. If you find yourself stuck in a rut or avoiding making the extra effort required to make an important change, take time out to analyze your goals for the future, realign your priorities to reflect your values, and, if necessary, seek spiritual direction to ensure that your values are aligned with God's will for you.

Outside support and a definitive plan with clear accountability can help the phlegmatic-sanguine to stay on track and motivated and can build his confidence to succeed.

We have discussed the various temperament combinations found in most individuals. Remember that no individual is completely locked into a specific form of behavior or action. Temperament does not reveal the whole person. A person is always more than his temperament or combination of temperaments. Through our free will, our character built over time through our moral choices, our attention to formation, and God's grace, we are each completely unique. Each of us is painting a picture or writing the book of our lives, and our temperament plays a small, although significant, part. Through learning about our temperament, we become more realistic about our own nature, more accepting of ourselves and others, and more capable of making prudent changes that will further us along the path toward holiness.

Chapter 10

∞

Temperament and the Spiritual Life

"God takes our humanness seriously."
Father Thomas Dubay

"But the fruit of the Spirit is love, joy,
peace, patience, kindness, goodness,
faithfulness, gentleness and self-control."
Galatians 5:22-23

∾

The desire for God is written in everyone's heart, because we are created by God and for God. As a result, we can never be truly happy until our hearts are centered on him. At times we are tempted to place our hope and trust in things of this world — money, status, power — or we may center our desires on other people or in our self-will. We may not at first know *what* will make us happy. But sooner or later we begin to realize, as St. Augustine wrote, "Our hearts are restless until they rest in thee, O Lord." So we embark on our quest, our search for God and for true happiness.

On our journey, we bring along our temperament — with its advantages and disadvantages. God's grace will supply whatever else we need. Since grace never destroys nature, but rather builds upon it and perfects it, it is critical to understand how our nature, specifically our temperament, affects our growth in the spiritual life. In this chapter, we will take a more detailed look at the inclinations that each temperament affords us with regard to prayer and the spiritual life. In addition, we will examine the characteristic spiritual weaknesses and temptations that can beset each temperament.

Human nature, created by God in his image, is essentially good. Yet as long as creation, wounded by Original Sin, is in a state of journeying toward perfection,[46] our temperaments are limited in the same way that all of nature is limited. Furthermore, our nature is wounded through Original Sin.

[46]CCC, 310.

The Temperament God Gave You

Many spiritual writers (such as St. Francis de Sales and Romano Guardini) stress that the imperfections that arise out of our natural temperament are not *culpable;* the weaknesses of our temperaments are not themselves sins. But they can make certain virtues more difficult to acquire. For example, some people are, by temperament, prone to sadness and find it extremely difficult to attain the virtue of magnanimity; others tend to be impulsive, and attaining the virtues of constancy and order is a true battle. Still others seem to be prone to action rather than to reflection.

The choleric temperament seems to possess almost naturally the virtue of magnanimity, while peacefulness and mildness seem quite difficult to attain. The sanguine naturally exhibits joy, yet must do battle to acquire self-control. The melancholic seems naturally capable of faithfulness (or long-suffering), while joy must be consciously acquired and prayed for. The phlegmatic is naturally quite gentle, yet perhaps needs to acquire the virtues of audacity and fortitude and to shed undue concern for the opinions of others. However, although imperfections may flow from our temperament, these can still be moderated or corrected by practice of the opposite virtue.[47] Nothing is impossible with God's grace.

∞

"Be perfect, as your heavenly
Father is perfect" (Matt. 5:48)

For baptized persons in a state of grace, the gifts of the Holy Spirit complete the natural (i.e., deriving from temperament) and acquired virtues. Charity, joy, peace, patience, kindness, goodness,

---

[47]Cf. St. Francis de Sales, *Introduction to the Devout Life* and Romano Guardini, *Learning the Virtues that Lead You to God*; also Jordan Aumann, O.P., *Spiritual Theology*.

generosity, gentleness, faithfulness, modesty, self-control, and chastity are perfections that the Holy Spirit forms in us, known as the "fruits" of the Holy Spirit.

Every Christian is called to holiness. Jesus gave us the new commandment, to love one another as he loved us. His love is a total, radical self-giving. Without God's grace, it would not be possible to imitate. But, with his grace and mercy, we can become the "living stones" that build his Church here on earth and help to bring about the coming of Christ's kingdom: "It is therefore quite clear that all Christians in any state or walk of life are called to the fullness of Christian life and to the perfection of love, and by this holiness, a more human manner of life is fostered also in earthly society."[48] All Christians — whatever their vocation, their state of life, or their temperament — are called to holiness.

∞

Transformation in Christ

Growth in the spiritual life is not merely a matter of adding a virtue or dropping a defect; it is not about harnessing a naturally virtuous temperament, or, conversely, about growing in virtue through great effort of the will; nor is it about self-perfection. It is, rather, a complete surrender to Christ, who draws us ever closer to him. This friendship with Christ requires us to change. It is not enough to follow Christ or to imitate him, but to be *transformed*.

We must be transformed, yet we remain essentially who we are. We don't start out human and become angels. Nor does God fashion us with a particular temperament, only to require us to become its opposite. Thus, if you are an enthusiastic, talkative sanguine, you will not necessarily be compelled to become a contemplative

[48]*Lumen Gentium*, 40.

monk with a vow of silence. A highly volatile and dynamic extravert is not likely to be transformed by grace into a complete introvert. He may, however, having learned to control his passions, become a highly enthusiastic Christ-centered leader noted for charity!

Father Marcial Maciel, founder of the Legionaries of Christ, writes that in our vocation to the Christian life, "Each person has his style, his gifts, his moment, his history, and consequently each one follows a mysterious path. . . . " He continues, "It is not easy to find your own method of prayer or the style of your relationship with God. In order to be more effective, you will have to modify and flexibly adapt the rhythm, style, and content of your prayer life and even the way you approach your spiritual program, depending on whether you are more emotional or more rational, more direct or more reflexive, more imaginative or more pragmatic, more sanguine or more phlegmatic."[49]

Knowing what our strengths and weaknesses are helps us to develop a plan for harnessing our strengths and avoiding our weaknesses — perhaps even eliminating them! If you are a very active choleric who wants to be a little more Mary (contemplative) and a little less Martha (active), you will realize that you need to set aside time every day to be still in the presence of the Lord. If you are a phlegmatic, you may wish to examine the purity of intention with which you undertake new activities, striving to do everything out of love for Christ, not merely because you don't want someone to get angry. If you are a melancholic struggling with the tendency to criticism, you can make a resolution at the beginning of each day to be generous and kind to co-workers and children, asking yourself each time a critical thought enters your mind, "How would Jesus see this person?"

[49]Letter 69, Envoy II.

The phlegmatic and sanguine are more relationship-oriented, likely to take into consideration people's feelings when making a decision, while the choleric and melancholic tend to make judgments based on harder facts and logic. This does not mean that people of any one temperament will have a greater or lesser ability to remain docile to the inspirations of the Holy Spirit or to order their faculties rightly. Nonetheless, as Father Thomas Dubay notes in *Authenticity*,[50] these two different approaches will have consequences in the spiritual life. Thus, we may find that the more affectively oriented sanguine may readily take direction from a trusted priest or spiritual director. A feeling-driven phlegmatic may find it easier to trust "inspirations" he receives from the Holy Spirit than a more skeptical choleric would. The more pragmatic, fact-oriented choleric may find himself seeking direction from the *Catechism of the Catholic Church* or by reading one of the great spiritual classics, but may find himself a tad reluctant to accept advice or direction from a young parish priest or a lay spiritual guide.

No matter what its source, we therefore strongly encourage seeking authentic spiritual direction as a means of guiding and focusing our natural tendencies toward service of Christ and the Church. So often it is tempting to surrender to our own whims and

---

[50]Father Dubay writes, "While there are people for whom the objective, out-there fact, rule, and norm are everything, there are others for whom their inner perception, feelings, and conscience are the ultimate criteria of truth. These differences among people are not to be viewed as unrelated to the problem of discerning the activities of the indwelling Spirit. If modern biblical and theological advances are teaching us anything, they are making it plain that God takes our humanness seriously" (Thomas Dubay, *Authenticity: A Biblical Theology of Discernment* [San Francisco: Ignatius Press, 1977], 84).

natural desires, to place ourselves at the center of the universe. But spiritual growth requires us to follow God's will instead of our own, and often we need help in discerning it. Discernment is a difficult and demanding task, and, whatever our natural temperament, we should be careful not to blithely or naively accept every inspiration as a revelation from God.[51] Scripture reminds us, "He who trusts in his own mind is a fool" (Prov. 28:26).

∞

Are some temperaments
better suited to sanctity?

There is no single temperament that is better able to progress in holiness. At first glance, you might suppose that the melancholic temperament, more naturally given to reflection and the interior life, must be more capable of achieving great holiness through contemplation or even mystical union with God. On the contrary, Father Adolphe Tanquerey, author of the classic *The Spiritual Life*, writes, "There have been and there are contemplatives of every temperament and of every condition of life." Everyone is called to holiness.

However, Father Tanquerey notes that "there are temperaments and modes of life which lend themselves better to infused contemplation. The reason for this is that contemplation is a free gift bestowed by God when and on whom he pleases, and that moreover, God is wont to adapt his graces to the temperament and the duties of state of each individual."[52]

---

[51] Ibid.

[52] Adolphe Tanquerey, *The Spiritual Life: A Treatise on Ascetical and Mystical Theology* (Rockford, Illinois: TAN Books, 2000), no. 1563.

⚭

Prayer and temperament

Unlike change on the natural level, transformation in the spirit is not simply a matter of buckling down and getting to work, although a firmly engaged will is necessary to change and grow spiritually. We are dependent on God's grace to be transformed: "Whoever remains in me and I in him will bear much fruit, because without me you can do nothing" (John 15:5).

Prayer is vitally necessary for every temperament. It is the humble recognition that we depend on God: for our existence, for our daily sustenance, for all good things. And so, we "lift our minds and hearts to God."[53] Jesus tells us, "Ask and you shall receive."

Not only do we ask for good things; we also seek intimacy and friendship with God. St. John Chrysostom writes, " 'As the deer longs for the running stream, so longs my soul for thee, O God,' writes the psalmist [Ps. 42]. The lover seeks the beloved, seeks union with him. Prayer is the light of the soul, giving us true knowledge of God. It is a link mediating between God and man. By prayer the soul is borne up to heaven and in a marvelous way embraces the Lord."[54]

Each temperament may also show some distinct preferences when it comes to forms of prayer.[55] The introverted melancholic

[53]CCC, par. 2559.

[54]Homily 6, *On Prayer*.

[55]In 1982, Chester Michael and Marie Norrisey surveyed 457 people on the relationship between prayer and personality type (using the MBTI and the Keirsey Temperament Sorter) and published their findings in *Prayer and Temperament* (Charlottesville: The Open Door, 1991). The discussion is useful if you are familiar with these personality tests.

may gravitate toward mental prayer, for example, while the extra-verted sanguine may find a prayer group naturally appealing. The practical and decisive choleric may be particularly uncomfortable if he finds himself in a very charismatic, feeling-oriented liturgical celebration. And so on.

However, some of the weaker areas of each temperament might be strengthened by learning another type of prayer, one that may not be as naturally appealing. For example, if you are a phleg-matic and you find yourself most comfortable with formalistic prayer (such as the Rosary, novenas, and so forth), perhaps you could develop your sensible imagination by trying the Ignatian form of meditation, in which you project yourself into the scrip-tural scene you are meditating on. If you're melancholic, you might find that a prayer group helps bring you out of yourself, stretches you, and provides you with opportunities to share with others the many blessings God has given you. Charismatic prayer may be completely foreign to your sharp and practical choleric's intellect, yet you may find it fruitful to mediate upon the words of Scripture and contemplate what the Holy Spirit is saying *to you right now.*

In any case, it is quite likely that, as we mature in our spiritual lives and deepen our personal relationship with Christ, we may find that our original preferences are less important. No matter what our particular temperament, we all should practice all the forms of prayer: adoration, petition, intercession, thanksgiving, and praise. It is just and proper for us to adore and thank our loving Father, who gives us all we need. And we must listen, too, for Christ, like any friend, isn't satisfied if we do nothing but ask for favors; he wants us to listen to him.

In addition to vocal (external) prayer, every Christian should make an effort to engage in mental (meditative and contemplative) prayer. Here, as the *Catechism* tells us, there are as many approaches as there are spiritual masters.[56]

Now let's take a more in-depth look at each of the temperament types from the spiritual vantage point.

We should note that many of the suggestions that follow are somewhat generic: *everyone* needs to have a strong prayer and sacramental life, to grow in virtue and in understanding of the will of God, and to nurture a personal relationship with Christ and an eagerness to serve him and his Church. As *Lumen Gentium* reminds us, we are all called to the perfection of love. For charity to grow in our souls like the good seed, we must willingly hear the word of God, carry out God's will in deeds, frequently receive the sacraments — especially the Eucharist — and apply ourselves assiduously to prayer, self-denial, brotherly service and growth in virtue.[57]

But within each temperament (or temperament combination), we find certain areas of strength and weakness. The following paragraphs will highlight particular spiritual practices that may be especially useful or may apply more readily to one temperament than another, given these strengths and weaknesses. If, like most people, you have a combination of temperaments (see the previous chapter), read the sections that apply to both your temperaments.

---

[56]CCC, 2707.
[57]*Lumen Gentium*, 42.

THE CHOLERIC'S SPIRITUAL LIFE
Moving faith from the head to the heart

Cholerics can be great saints . . . or great sinners. Once they perceive a goal, they will wholeheartedly pursue it. The key is pursuing the right goal! A choleric without a spiritual life, or one who is totally living on the natural level, is likely to be passionate, driven, prideful — even cruel and violent — in the pursuit of his goals. When these goals are not God-given, much damage can occur. Consider St. Paul, who is thought to have been of choleric temperament. Prior to his conversion, Saul was rabidly anti-Christian, "laying waste" to the Church, dragging off the early followers and throwing them into prison (Acts 8:3). But, after his encounter with Christ, he became even more fervent in spreading the gospel; becoming, perhaps, the greatest apostle.

St. James must have been a choleric. One of the "Sons of Thunder," he was a man of action, ambition, and strong words — not to mention temper. When the Samaritan village did not welcome Jesus, James (with John) asked, "Lord, do you want us to call down fire from heaven to consume them?" (Luke 9:54). With John, he wanted to sit in a position of glory at the right or the left hand of Jesus (Mark 10:37).

Cholerics are neither joiners nor followers, preferring always to lead, and they are not naturally docile to direction. But they must learn to follow Christ. Without a spiritual director, the choleric tends to do his own will, and will assume that he's right — even when he's *very* wrong.

Stubborn attachment to his own ideas and his own will ("my way or the highway") might cause difficulty for the choleric in his personal relationships and might contribute to a certain lack of docility in taking spiritual direction. The choleric will tend to question, argue, and debate everything first. This doesn't necessarily mean that he is wedded to his oppositional position; rather, it means he needs to feel he has come to assent or agreement freely, using his own reason. An astute spiritual director will offer guidance without seeming to infringe on the strong will of the choleric, respecting the choleric's strong need to come to a decision on his own.

> **CHOLERIC**
>
> **Spiritual gifts:** Zeal for souls, fortitude, knowledge.
>
> **Spiritual weaknesses:** Self-will, control, anger, haughtiness, superiority.
>
> **Saint who shares your temperament:** St. Paul.

If you are a choleric, you might have observed this in yourself: someone asks you to do something, and your first reaction is to question his judgment and to think you have a better way of doing it. A choleric who has never struggled to attain the virtue of docility may prove to be quite a thorn in the side of his boss, spiritual director, or church group! But once you become aware of this tendency, you can work through your initial temptation to question and argue, and strive to be a team player, exemplifying docility to your directors or boss for the sake of *esprit de corps* and the common good. To develop the virtue of charity, you may have to sacrifice your strong attachment to self-will and develop your desire for unity, self-sacrifice, graciousness, and kindness.

Your active and decisive temperament will lead you naturally toward the apostolate. Perhaps your pastor or members of your parish will call upon your assistance in parish projects or in larger diocesan initiatives. Your leadership ability and enthusiasm are usually recognizable. You might even find yourself juggling many projects at once. As a result, you may be a candidate for activism — doing too many things without a supernatural spirit. When

Peter didn't pray with Jesus in the Garden of Gethsemane, he resorted to violent action (cutting off the soldier's ear), and Jesus reprimanded him. God does not want action divorced from prayer. Remember the Benedictine motto *"Ora et labora"* ("Pray and work"); work alone will never suffice in the spiritual realm.

It is worthwhile for you to meditate on the Mystical Body of Christ. The body of Christ has many parts; one individual cannot do it all, nor is your way the *only* way. While you are actively participating in building up the Church, reflect upon the importance of unity and charity. Without a deep and abiding prayer life, you risk blind activism, the egotism of individualism, or an apostolate founded on pride and vanity rather than on the pure love of Jesus Christ. Prayer is vital.

Frequent reception of the sacraments, especially Holy Communion and Confession, is also critical. Pope John Paul II tells us, "Every commitment to holiness, every activity aimed at carrying out the Church's mission, every work of pastoral planning must draw the strength it needs from the Eucharistic mystery and in turn be directed to that mystery as its culmination. In the Eucharist we have Jesus, we have his redemptive sacrifice, we have his Resurrection, we have the gift of the Holy Spirit, we have adoration, obedience, and love of the Father. Were we to disregard the Eucharist, how could we overcome our own deficiency?"[58]

Distraction in prayer plagues all temperaments. For the choleric, it may be due to the fact that you always have many items on your "to do" list, and you want to waste no time getting started on them. You may find yourself distracted by pressing agenda items and want to spring immediately into action on those tasks.

---

[58]John Paul II, Encyclical *Ecclesia de Eucharistia* (May 2003), www.vatican.va.

Instead, keep a pad of paper near your spiritual reading or place of prayer and, when distractions arise, simply jot them down. Then you can return to prayer, assured that the tasks, not forgotten, will still be there when you are done. Elijah was thinking like a choleric when he expected the Lord to be in the earthquake or the violent wind (1 Kings 19:11-13). Like Elijah, you need to wait and listen, and hear the Lord in the gentle whisper in your heart.

Another temptation you might experience is to remain emotionally detached from your prayer. The intellectual stimulation of spiritual reading can appear to provide spiritual consolation — so much so that you do not move from your head to your heart. It is vital that you go more deeply into meditation to the point that your prayer becomes a prayer of the *heart*. We recommend using Scripture as your source of meditation, as well as challenging spiritual writers who are able to draw their readers into a deeper relationship with Christ or more deeply into prayer.

THE MELANCHOLIC'S SPIRITUAL LIFE
Longing for heaven

It is said that a melancholic so longs for heaven that he can never be happy with less than perfection here on earth. Even as small children, melancholics are concerned with truth, beauty, and justice. They are naturally inclined toward reflection, prayer, and piety. They are compassionate, intelligent, and introspective, which are great assets in the spiritual life and may explain why it is often thought that the saints who achieved the heights of contemplation were melancholics.

If a melancholic is not aware of this intense spiritual longing for perfection, he might find himself extremely dissatisfied and frustrated on the natural level, without knowing why. Deep intimacy with God in prayer and good spiritual guidance will be able to help him avoid a downward cycle of frustration, anxiety, and depression.

It is often said that St. Paul was a choleric who had strong melancholic tendencies. He exhibited the intelligence, deep prayer life (even mystical experiences), and the striving for perfection of the melancholic. He wrote that he was "caught up to the third heaven." And "I know that this person (whether in the body or out of the body I do not know, God knows) was caught up into Paradise and heard ineffable things" (2 Cor. 12:3-4). Once while preaching, he spoke on and on, until midnight, refusing to take into account his audience (until a young man drifted off to sleep and fell out the window!), just as a preachy melancholic would (Acts 20:7-12). At another point, Paul separated from Barnabus and John, known as Mark, because Mark had deserted them at Pamphylia, thus indicating his long memory when it came to a personal grievance (Acts 15:37-38).

Melancholics are slow to respond to stimuli and can seem to be irresolute. Fear of the future can also stymie their activity. Spiritual writers have pointed out that melancholics take a long time to decide about a vocation to the religious life. Sometimes melancholics will balk at committing to the apostolate, sometimes out of fear of potential failure or anxiety about details.

If you are a melancholic, you may find yourself flooded by thoughts of potential disasters or difficulties — all piling up at once in your consciousness. *This project will be a disaster! I cannot possibly undertake this apostolate!* You may be paralyzed by anxiety or by fear of failure. Even worse, you may fear that you cannot grow in holiness! You may become overwhelmed by critical thoughts, scrupulously reviewing your past mistakes. Always bring such feelings of scrupulosity to a spiritual director, for it is a very real problem in the spiritual life.

When you find yourself flooded by thoughts of potential disaster, learn to put those negative thoughts out of your mind immediately, developing the trust in God that you need to take a leap of faith and commit generously to serving Christ. "With God all things are possible," could be your motto.

Another great stumbling block for the melancholic is self-pity — a tendency that can result in isolation, self-centeredness, envy, and possibly even depression. To gain joy, you should reflect in thanksgiving on all the gifts the Lord has given you. Say prayers of thanksgiving, especially for specific gifts and blessings. "Rejoice in the Lord always," St. Paul tells us,

---

MELANCHOLIC

Spiritual gifts: Piety, long-suffering, wisdom.

Spiritual weaknesses: Timidity, scrupulosity, judgmentalism, despair.

Saint who shares your temperament: St. Teresa Benedicta of the Cross (Edith Stein).

"whatever is true, whatever is honorable, whatever is just, whatever is pure, whatever is lovely, whatever is gracious, if there is any excellence and if there is anything worthy of praise, think about these things" (Phil. 4:8). Melancholics should take St. Paul's advice literally: *think* about these things! There lies an antidote to crankiness and a recipe for joy!

Without a strong spiritual life (and the melancholic may overtly desire this more than any of the other temperaments), the melancholic can become resentful, bitter, and despairing at worst, or negative and judgmental at best. Melancholics have a natural tendency to moodiness, which can be exacerbated by their thought processes. They should try to become aware of how their thoughts contribute to their moods and, when a negative mood begins, or negative thoughts creep in, should immediately refocus their attention on the underlying positives, as St. Paul recommends.

My melancholic friend Mary Beth reminds herself that she must learn to embrace suffering and, at the same time, realize that it is not as bad as she thinks. To help in this regard, she will "label" the suffering and then try to look at it objectively; and she often finds that the label reveals that it's not as dreadful as she had hitherto thought, especially when she's in one of her melancholic dark moods. She finds that she can pull herself out of any pity-party by taking the aerial view, asking herself, "*In the scope of things,* how bad is this?" This helps her gain perspective and pull herself out of small-mindedness, like a mole coming out of his hole to take a look around at the many far more serious sufferings others experience.

So that we will not be discouraged or lose heart, St. Paul advises us to keep in mind our *ultimate goal* — heaven — and our ultimate union with the *beloved,* Jesus Christ: "We are afflicted in every way, but not constrained; perplexed, but not driven to despair; persecuted, but not abandoned; struck down but not destroyed. . . . For we who live are constantly being given up to death for the sake of Jesus" (2 Cor. 4:7-12). "Therefore we are not discouraged. . . . For this momentary light affliction is producing for us an eternal weight of glory beyond comparison, as we look not to what is seen but to what is unseen" (2 Cor. 4:16-18).

A strong spiritual life, with frequent reception of the sacraments and an intimate relationship with Christ, will help dispel the feelings of depression that can afflict the melancholic.[59] During the eighteenth International Conference on Depression in 2003, Pope John Paul II noted that depression is always a *spiritual trial* and recommended meditation on the Psalms, "in which the holy author expresses his joys and anxieties in prayer"; the recitation of the Rosary to see Christ with Mary's eyes; and participation in the Eucharist, "source of interior peace."[60]

Pride, in the melancholic, does not usually manifest itself as an attempt to gain recognition or honor, as it might in a choleric. The melancholic does not seek overt praise or commendation. However, the melancholic does fear failure! Thus, his pride shows up in his desire to be perfect and in his fear of disgrace. In his pursuit of "perfection," he begins to strive to do everything equally perfectly: regarding the home, the kids, and the apostolate. A melancholic may have a hard time prioritizing, because he wants to do everything perfectly! If you're a melancholic, make sure that your own high ideals don't result in a lack of empathy for those who do not have equally high ideals or who need to be motivated or taught (such as children!).

---

[59] If you are experiencing any of the signs of clinical depression, always seek qualified psychological help.

[60] November 14, 2003 audience.

Melancholics can be tempted to hold everyone, including themselves, to an impossibly high standard. A melancholic who loses sight of his ultimate goal can become a real cross to himself as well as to his spouse and children — critiquing, complaining, and constantly seeking that elusive goal of "perfection." He can appear very self-effacing and humble, but when he works on a project, he becomes so critical and exacting that no one else feels competent enough to collaborate on the project! His co-workers give up, feeling as if they have done a poor job. In the end, the melancholic is alone, over-burdened, and resentful. In such a way, pride can seep in to destroy spiritual fruits.

A melancholic needs to develop a greater acceptance and appreciation of the foibles of human nature and to learn not to sweat the small stuff. A deep spiritual life, particularly an intimate relationship with Jesus Christ, will help him realize that only Jesus Christ is the true and perfect friend of his soul. No earthly human being can ever satisfy our deepest longings for intimacy — to be perfectly understood and unconditionally loved. Only a deep, personal relationship with Christ will answer these needs, and with it, the melancholic will become less self-absorbed, less demanding and critical of others, and more gentle, forgiving, and genuinely appreciative.

If you are a melancholic, a virtue you might find particularly beneficial to develop is optimism, or supernatural hope. Optimism, when founded on confidence in God, gives us inner peace and supernatural joy. As a virtue, it requires us to be realistic and seek positive aspects in every situation, including difficult ones. If you are a melancholic, trustful surrender to Divine Providence will give you peace and joy.

You should also place a high priority on delicate charity toward your neighbor. There is a temptation to value *truth* so highly that it trumps charity. Many a melancholic has complained, "But God doesn't want us to be untruthful! True charity is charity toward God!" This is a false dilemma. Charity is also in the small details: in the *way* you tell someone the truth, for instance. You must express appreciation for others. It will require a firm commitment of your will to do it (for you do not naturally feel like doing this): overtly and consciously to extend kindness toward others and express your sincere gratitude and appreciation for all those in your life. See Christ in everyone!

A melancholic, whose natural inclination is to strive for the ideal, may err in making "perfection" his ultimate goal — perfection in achieving holiness. Although all persons are called to holiness, holiness for its own sake is not our ultimate goal; rather, union with God is our ultimate goal, and, with God's grace, we must become holy to achieve it!

The Temperament God Gave You

THE SANGUINE'S SPIRITUAL LIFE
Rejoice in the Lord always!

Sanguines are quick to react, but not long to remember — naturally gifted with the virtue of forgiveness! They are extraverted, devoted, and life-loving, and have great people skills.

St. Peter was a lovable sanguine. "I will never betray you, Lord!" he promises. Then, when questioned, he goes along with the crowd: "No, I am not one of them!" (Luke 22:58). At the Transfiguration, he enthusiastically offers, "Let us set up three tents!" Even though, as Scripture also notes, "he did not know what he was saying" (Luke 9:33). He impetuously jumps out of the boat to walk on the water, but then looks down at the water and, afraid, begins to sink (Matt. 14:30). He falls asleep in the Garden of Olives and then impulsively cuts off the Roman's ear (John 18:10). Peter tells Christ that he will never let him suffer and die; Jesus says, "Get behind me, Satan" (Mark 8:27-33). St. Peter was the one to whom the vision was given to spread the Faith among the Gentiles and who brought the first Gentile into the Church. He was also the one to first work a miracle after Pentecost. His openness and generosity and love for people may have contributed to these "firsts."

St. Philip Neri was probably a lively and joyful sanguine. He was "a handsome boy with attractive manners and a gay spirit, but sensitive — the kind that quickly wins affection from others."[61] He was not overly pious as a child and was perhaps a bit impulsive (noted at his canonization was the time he pushed his sister because she interrupted him, and the time he tore up a copy of the

[61] V. J. Matthews, *St. Philip Neri* (Rockford, Illinois: TAN Books, 1984).

family tree). He was a practical joker, but used his humor to gain souls for Christ. "I will have no melancholy, no low spirits in my house," he was known to say.

Relationships are important to the sanguine; he is very adept at dealing with people and is naturally considerate and responsive. But his temptation is to place his trust *solely* in other people, even to the point of denying what he knows to be right in order to please someone important to him. A sanguine should follow a program of life that includes placing his trust in God first and foremost, strengthening his personal relationship with Christ, and developing *control* over his emotions, and *consistency* and *perseverance* in his spiritual resolutions.

> **SANGUINE**
>
> **Spiritual gifts:** Joy, mercy, magnanimity, gratitude.
>
> **Spiritual weaknesses:** Self-love, envy, seeking esteem and human respect.
>
> **Saint who shares your temperament:** St. Peter.

The sanguine is very eager to serve Christ and the Church; but if he undertakes many projects without sufficient reflection or prayer, he might find himself quickly overloaded, with little time to accomplish anything well. In prayer, he may become distracted. In such cases, as well as in times of aridity or lack of consolation, the sanguine should practice perseverance out of love for God.

The sanguine is docile and cooperative in groups, so religious communities are often formed of sanguines (and phlegmatics; it is the melancholic or choleric who might actually *found* an order). Sanguines are active and work well with other people; they are a joy to have in an apostolic activity. Because they value relationships, they might find a prayer group or a Cursillo weekend inspiring and helpful. But they can also be easily misled by unscrupulous persons. Therefore, it is critical for the sanguine to have good spiritual direction and to develop spiritual discernment skills.

If you are a lively, imaginative sanguine who struggles to stay focused on prayer, you might find that praying in an atmosphere that capitalizes on your active sensibilities — for example, in a beautiful church with lighted candles, incense, stained-glass windows, or ornate statuary — will be greatly beneficial. The Ignatian form of meditation, which allows you to place yourself in your imagination at the very Gospel scene you are meditating on, might also be very profitable.

If you are struggling with constancy, you might particularly benefit by meditating on the Passion. The authors of *Prayer and Temperament* offer this recommendation (among others) for those with very active senses and imagination: "Take your crucifix, look intently at it, feel it, kiss it. In your imagination, go back to the first Good Friday. Try to put yourself in the place of Jesus being nailed to the Cross. This is what St. Francis did in the cave at Alverno. . . . "[62]

In spiritual studies, the sanguine might be tempted to settle for a cursory or superficial understanding. He may find it difficult to stay focused in performing apostolic work: flitting from task to task, depending on what appeals to him at the time, never following through with perseverance. But this can be remedied with motivation. If the sanguine is motivated by love for Christ, and is given good direction, structure, and formation, he will be a zealous and joyful apostle for the Lord!

[62]Michael and Norrisey do not make their prayer recommendations based on the classic four temperaments, but instead are focusing on the Myers-Briggs Temperament Indicator; however, this particular suggestion seems quite applicable to the sanguine temperament.

Temperament and the Spiritual Life

If you are sanguine, it is important to develop both depth and constancy in your spiritual life. Christ calls you to leave the shallows and go deeper: *Duc in altum!* (Luke 5:4). One way to encourage this is to make reflection a habit; make it a policy to *think* before you act. When you meditate on the Scriptures, do not be satisfied with the warm glow of inspired thoughts while reading; go deeper, and make a resolution based on what Christ is asking of you. Check up on yourself at night during your examination of conscience.

A prayer group that also requires accountability in fulfilling prayer commitments and spiritual formation will help you develop self-discipline in the spiritual life. Taking part in a movement or a spirituality that meets regularly with evenings of reflection or for prayer and study will be extremely helpful. A spiritual director will also help you achieve discipline and commitment.

If you are a sanguine who was raised at a time when very little substance was covered in religious education, or if your parents were somewhat oblivious of the effects of the culture on your formation, or you had only the minimum of religious instruction, you might find yourself discouraged and might feel spiritually insecure, rely on others' opinions, or blame your parents or history for your formation gaps. The truth is, we are all responsible for our own spiritual formation, simply by our incorporation into the Church! We should not blame our parents or our teachers. The antidote to this spiritual insecurity is to develop self-discipline in the spiritual life, a discipline that includes daily prayer as well as self-formation through spiritual reading and through growth in virtue. Tackle one virtue at a time, if you feel you are very far behind.

Through prayer and a close relationship with Christ, you will come to understand your depth as a unique individual and will begin to root your confidence in the basis for all true confidence:

The Temperament God Gave You

God's absolute unconditional love for you. You will begin to appreciate your strengths and to attack your weaknesses. When you make an effort to practice mental prayer, and to know the person of Jesus Christ intimately through meditation on the scriptures, you will discover great depths within yourself — depths you did not realize you had — along with a great capacity for self-sacrifice, a generosity in self-giving, and the joyous heart of a true apostle. Your vivacity, joy, devotion, and sensitivity will draw many other souls to Christ and will help build up the Church.

THE PHLEGMATIC'S SPIRITUAL LIFE
Blessed are the meek

St. Thomas Aquinas is thought to have been a brilliant phlegmatic. Neither excitable nor loquacious, like the sanguine and choleric temperaments, he was careful in speech and thought and detached, dispassionate, and methodical in his arguments. His temperament served him well as a philosopher: he thought things through deeply and thoroughly, never rushing to conclusions or letting emotion get in the way of his reason.

Adaptable in groups, friendly, and respectful of authority and tradition, phlegmatics have long been considered excellent members of religious communities. They are gentle, quietly persevering, and faithful. With attention to self-formation and motivation on the human level, they can also be superb leaders. Our pastor is a great leader who is phlegmatic. But he has a deep prayer life, is assiduous in his continued spiritual self-formation, seeks intellectually stimulating reading, and listens to motivational tapes every morning! Phlegmatics are very principled as well. They are true to their word and value honesty and integrity.

On the other hand, because of their cooperative spirit and their fear of conflict, they might be tempted to compromise their principles and go along with the status quo. Phlegmatics have a tendency to laziness, and without spiritual formation and motivation, they can become spiritual couch potatoes. They might also be tempted to do things that please other people, instead of God. They might not, on their own, gravitate toward spiritual practices that seem arduous — even something simple, such as a holy hour. But if the structure is provided and they find the initial motivation, they will be faithful to their commitments. But the motivation to get there in the first place is critical.

If you are a phlegmatic, don't sell yourself short! Audacity is a virtue founded in prudence, yet with a strong passion for noble ideals and great undertakings. In your spiritual program, work on building confidence in Christ, fortitude, and prudence. Meeting Christ in prayer each and every morning, in a spiritual communion during the day, and again in an examination of conscience in the evening will help combat any temptation to spiritual laziness.

PHLEGMATIC

Spiritual gifts: Peace, understanding, counsel, meekness.

Spiritual weaknesses: Sensuality, sloth, complacency.

Saint who shares your temperament: St. Thomas Aquinas.

You might be attracted to formulaic prayers, such as the Rosary, the Liturgy of the Hours, and the Divine Mercy Chaplet. Sacramentals might also be very appealing to you, especially the brown scapular and the Miraculous Medal. Do not stop with externals or devotions, however. Take a more active role in prayer by engaging your imagination. Place yourself in a scene from the Gospels, noting how you feel and what the Holy Spirit is telling you. Perhaps you are a shepherd boy near the manger where Jesus lay, as the Blessed Mother gently rocked him and the Magi adored him. Does the infant Jesus look at you? How do you feel? Even one tear shed by the Son of God as an infant could have saved mankind!

Prayer journals and prayer groups are also very helpful, providing the encouragement to vocalize your insights from the Holy Spirit, and also the structure and predictability that phlegmatics enjoy. A prayer group or a parish society will also provide some necessary encouragement, motivation, accountability and reinforcement to keep the fire blazing.

Watch out for the tendency to avoid the necessary struggle of the spiritual life. Meditating on the parable of the talents will not only highlight the gifts God has given you, but also remind you of the responsibility such gifts carry with them. Do not bury your talents! Phlegmatics will flourish with commitment to a structure with accountability. Ongoing commitment to parish life, serving the Church within a clearly identifiable structure (as opposed to just helping out when you feel like it), spiritual direction, regular prayer groups, and other spiritual activities that promote service of the Church within a supportive environment will be extremely beneficial.

The Temperament God Gave You

∽

Know yourself, and begin to know God

Spiritual growth will always entail a deep prayer life and a humble submission to God's will, lived out in charity. As one spiritual author says, holiness is in the will, because if we love God, we will surely end up with him.[63] But we will be able to love God better if we know him and if we know ourselves. God is constant, and we are not. God loves unconditionally, and we do not. God is always faithful, but we are not. If we are aware of our own foibles and natural tendencies, we will be better able to thwart those failings and tendencies to sin that spring from our own inclinations, wounded by Original Sin. As the eminent Swiss theologian Hans Urs Von Balthasar wrote, "We men are not in the least aware of the proportions and impact of our guilt."[64]

The more we grasp reality, understanding ourselves and others, the greater our love for God will be and the greater our love for all members of the Body of Christ. As St. Paul tells us, "at present we see indistinctly, as in a mirror, but then face-to-face. At present I know partially; then I shall know fully as I am fully known" (1 Cor. 13:12). At present we seek God's face and our own, we want to live in the light, but we must make an effort to grow in wisdom and holiness, just as the child Jesus did. Ultimately, love is the only path: "So faith, hope, and love remain, these three; but the greatest of these is love" (1 Cor. 13:13).

---

[63]Frank Sheed, *Theology and Sanity* (San Francisco: Ignatius Press, 1978).

[64]Hans Urs Von Balthasar, *Heart of the World,* trans. Erasmo S. Leiva (San Francisco: Ignatius Press, 1979).

∞

Temperament Indicator

⚮

Check the boxes below that describe your *habitual* tendencies, the *pattern* of reaction evident from childhood, with regard to each of the following qualities. Do not select qualities that you would like to have or that you are required to have on the job. Choose those qualities that most often apply to you, that your spouse or best friends would say you have, the qualities you most often gravitate toward in times of ease or resort to in times of stress, and even those less positive tendencies you are trying to avoid.

1. ❑ I react quickly when presented with an idea, a person, or a situation

2. ❑ I react slowly when presented with an idea, a person, or a situation

3. ❑ I react strongly (in intensity) when presented with an idea, a person, or a situation

4. ❑ I do not react intensely when presented with an idea, a person, or a situation

5. ❑ I want to take immediate action on an idea, in a situation, or with a person

6. ❑ When presented with an idea, a person, or a situation, I remain calm and wait to react

7. ❑ I do not react initially, but my reaction grows steadily in intensity

8. ❑ Impressions last a long time

9. ❑ Impressions last a short time

10. ❑ Accepting

11. ❑ Adventurous

12. ❑ "Worry wart"

13. ❑ Introspective

14. ❑ Easily provoked

15. ❑ If provoked, will retaliate

16. ❑ Serious

17. ❑ Appreciate flattery

18. ❑ Inclined to flatter

19. ❑ Careful

20. ❑ Inward

21. ❑ Introverted

22. ❑ Eye for detail

23. ❑ Distractible

24. ❑ Prone to reflection

25. ❑ Determined

26. ❑ Trusting

27. ❑ Grudging

28. ❑ Detached

29. ❑ Love company

30. ❑ Enjoy people

31. ❑ Doubtful

32. ❑ People-oriented

33. ❑ Annoyed by disorder

34. ❑ Abhor injustice

35. ❑ Fair

36. ❑ Easily angered

37. ❑ Enthusiastic

38. ❑ Extraverted

39. ❑ Loner

40. ❑ Skeptical

41. ❑ Center of attention

42. ❑ Revengeful

43. ❑ Exaggerate easily

44. ❑ Self-professed leader

45. ❑ Servant-leader

46. ❑ Charismatic

47. ❑ Envious

48. ❑ Jealous

49. ❑ Happy

50. ❑ Optimistic

51. ❑ Prone to illness

52. ❑ Easily discouraged

53. ❑ Bullheaded

54. ❏ Rational

55. ❏ Diplomatic

56. ❏ Tend to blurt things out

57. ❏ Suspicious

58. ❏ Peaceful

59. ❏ Creative

60. ❏ Take charge

61. ❏ Patient

62. ❏ Second-guessing

63. ❏ Love peace and quiet

64. ❏ Dutiful

65. ❏ Hate conflict

66. ❏ Love to debate

67. ❏ Argumentative

68. ❏ Sentimental

69. ❏ Crowd-pleaser

70. ❏ Slow to warm up

71. ❏ Make friends easily

72. ❏ Reticent

73. ❏ Logical

74. ❏ Pondering

75. ❏ Love silence

76. ❏ Fashionable

77. ❏ Enjoy parties

78. ❏ Prefer to be alone

79. ❏ Artistic

80. ❏ Poetic

81. ❏ Thinker

82. ❏ Talkative

83. ❏ Abhor sentimentality

84. ❏ Not empathetic

85. ❏ Rule-oriented

86. ❏ Persevering

87. ❏ Flirtatious

88. ❏ Reserved

89. ❏ Easily slip into gossip

90. ❏ Always right

91. ❏ Looks are important

92. ❏ Idea person

93. ❏ Lack follow-through

94. ❏ Love variety

95. ❏ Affectionate

96. ❏ Not affectively demonstrative

97. ❏ Indifferent

98. ❏ Wavering

99. ❏ Hard to please

100. ❏ Sober and practical

101. ❏ Moody

102. ❏ Composed

103. ❏ Deliberate

104. ❏ Prankster

105. ❏ Obstinate

106. ❏ Pessimistic

107. ❏ Tolerant

108. ❏ Courageous

109. ❏ Timid

110. ❏ "Forgive and forget"

111. ❏ "Let's wait and see"

112. ❏ Hotheaded

113. ❏ Prefer to follow

114. ❏ Rash

115. ❏ Intense

116. ❏ Quick-tempered

117. ❏ Frank

118. ❏ Impatient

119. ❏ Even-keeled

120. ❏ Flighty

121. ❏ Glass half-full

122. ❏ Glass half-empty

123. ❏ Bulldozer

124. ❏ "Strike while the iron is hot"

125. ❏ Loose cannon

126. ❏ Polite

127. ❏ Easily aroused to debate

128. ❏ Inwardly peaceful

129. ❏ Good-natured

130. ❏ Interruptive

131. ❏ In tune with others' feelings

132. ❏ Strong-willed

133. ❏ Contrary

134. ❏ Fearless

135. ❏ Ambitious

136. ❏ Cheerful

137. ❏ Self-composed

138. ❏ Action-oriented

139. ❏ Comfortable being a part of a group

140. ❏ Prefer to take charge of a group

141. ❏ Dislike groups

142. ❏ Joiner

143. ❏ Quick and decisive

144. ❏ Robust

145. ❏ Cordial

146. ❑ Enjoy change

147. ❑ Prefer routine

148. ❑ Open and sociable

149. ❑ Curious

150. ❑ Critical

151. ❑ Focus on problems

152. ❑ Impulsive

153. ❑ Methodical

154. ❑ Bold

155. ❑ Take initiative

156. ❑ Insistent upon own plan

157. ❑ Self-confident

158. ❑ Self-reliant

159. ❑ Sensitive

160. ❑ Easily hurt

161. ❑ Tendency to skim surface

162. ❑ Adaptive

163. ❑ Reclusive

164. ❑ Self-conscious

165. ❑ Overcautious

166. ❑ Tends to discouragement

167. ❑ Exclusive

168. ❑ Private

169. ❏ Mediator

170. ❏ Indecisive

171. ❏ Constant

172. ❏ Competitive

173. ❏ Self-sacrificing

174. ❏ Respectful

175. ❏ Adaptable

176. ❏ Analytical

177. ❏ Persistent

178. ❏ Playful

179. ❏ Laugh easily

180. ❏ Spontaneous

181. ❏ Hesitant

182. ❏ Scheduled

183. ❏ Outspoken

184. ❏ Orderly

185. ❏ Obliging

186. ❏ Faithful

187. ❏ Idealistic

188. ❏ Inoffensive

189. ❏ Dry wit

190. ❏ Deep

191. ❏ Mover

192. ❏ Motivator

193. ❏ Attentive to others

194. ❏ Bossy

195. ❏ Well-behaved

196. ❏ Willful

197. ❏ Perfectionist

198. ❏ Peacekeeper

199. ❏ Dispassionate

200. ❏ Controlling

201. ❏ Calm under fire

202. ❏ Spiritual

203. ❏ Love excitement

204. ❏ Thoughtful

205. ❏ Procrastinating

206. ❏ Docile

207. ❏ Headstrong

208. ❏ Require rest

209. ❏ Demand acknowledgment

210. ❏ Need encouragement

211. ❏ Need motivating

212. ❏ Need friends

213. ❏ Focused and intense

214. ❏ Need fun

215. ❏ Enjoy structure, procedures

216. ❏ Need uplifting

217. ❏ Non-confrontative

218. ❏ Confrontative

219. ❏ Pragmatic

220. ❏ Mercurial

221. ❏ Wary of new situations

222. ❏ Singularly focused

223. ❏ Like to shop and eat out

224. ❏ Driven

225. ❏ Will subjugate own desires to please others

226. ❏ Process-oriented

227. ❏ Goal-oriented

228. ❏ Comfortable in present moment

229. ❏ Future oriented

230. ❏ A social butterfly

231. ❏ Jokester

232. ❏ Homebody

SCORING

Now circle below the numbers you checked, and add up the total number of circles for each temperament. The highest total should indicate your primary temperament, and the next highest will be a strong indicator of your secondary temperament.

Choleric: 1, 3, 5, 8, 11, 14, 15, 25, 30, 36, 37, 38, 42, 43, 44, 50, 53, 54, 56, 60, 66, 67, 73, 81, 83, 84, 86, 90, 92, 96, 105, 108, 112, 115, 116, 117, 118, 121, 123, 124, 125, 127, 130, 132, 133, 134, 135, 138, 140, 143, 144, 154, 155, 156, 157, 158, 167, 168, 172, 176, 177, 183, 191, 192, 194, 196, 200, 207, 209, 213, 218, 219, 222, 224, 227

Sanguine: 1, 3, 5, 9, 10, 11, 14, 17, 18, 23, 26, 29, 30, 32, 36, 37, 38, 41, 43, 46, 47, 48, 49, 50, 56, 59, 68, 69, 71, 76, 77, 79, 80, 82, 87, 89, 91, 92, 93, 94, 95, 104, 107, 110, 112, 113, 114, 116, 117, 118, 120, 121, 129, 131, 136, 138, 139, 142, 144, 145, 146, 148, 149, 152, 157, 159, 160, 161, 175, 178, 179, 180, 203, 206, 212, 214, 220, 223, 226, 228, 230, 231

Melancholic: 2, 7, 8, 12, 13, 16, 19, 20, 21, 22, 24, 27, 28, 31, 33, 34, 39, 40, 42, 48, 51, 52, 54, 57, 62, 63, 70, 72, 73, 74, 75, 78, 79, 80, 81, 88, 98, 99, 101, 106, 109, 111, 122, 131, 133, 141, 150, 151, 153, 159, 163, 165, 166, 170, 173, 176, 181, 182, 184, 186, 187, 190, 193, 197, 202, 204, 208, 210, 215, 216, 221, 222, 227

Phlegmatic: 2, 4, 6, 9, 10, 21, 26, 28, 30, 31, 35, 39, 45, 52, 55, 58, 61, 63, 64, 65, 68, 70, 72, 75, 78, 85, 88, 97, 98, 100, 102, 103, 106, 107, 110, 111, 113, 119, 122, 126, 128, 129, 131, 137, 139, 147, 153, 160, 162, 166, 169, 171, 173, 174, 175, 185, 186, 188, 189, 195, 198, 199, 201, 204, 205, 206, 210, 211, 215, 217, 219, 221, 225, 226, 228, 232

QUALITIES OF THE
FOUR TEMPERAMENTS

Choleric

Quick to react, intense reaction of long duration; leader; initiator; logical; pragmatic, person of action, forthright; pushes plans through; doesn't display emotions easily, except anger; not given to anxiety; impetuous; eager to express himself; loves debate; can be defensive and prideful; persevering; self-confident; self-reliant; not a follower; driven to achieve goals; private; inclined to retaliation; extraverted; take-charge; argumentative; abhors sentimentality; logical; goal-oriented; decisive; intense; quick-tempered; optimistic; interruptive; needs acknowledgment; wants to be right; a doer; headstrong; competitive; looks for the positive; impatient; productive; makes decisions based on principles/ideas.

Melancholic

Slow to react, with intense reaction growing over time and of long duration; thoughtful; spiritual; deep; poetic; introverted; overly cautious; perfectionist; thinker; critical; doesn't prioritize well; tends to discouragement and self-pity; worries over possible misfortune; can be a hypochondriac; easily hurt; slow and sometimes indecisive; pessimistic; moody; goal-oriented; detached from environment; few friends; exclusive; likes to be alone; second-guesses; introspective; holds grudges; abhors injustice; is motivated by problems; looks at the down side; idealistic; self-sacrificing; sensitive; makes decisions based on principles/ideas.

Sanguine

Quick to react; reactions of short duration; relationship-oriented; doesn't hold grudges; life of the party; funny; loves to be with people; optimistic; likes groups; talkative; popular; docile; follower; seldom embarrassed; loves variety; attuned to environment; likes clothes; can be faddish; enjoys shopping and eating out; high energy; quick to forgive; welcomes change; frank; talkative; sociable; less interested in follow-through; can be superficial; cordial; makes friends easily; self-assured; carefree; eager; likes to talk in front of groups; enthusiastic; prone to vanity; artistic and creative; spontaneous; sometimes forgetful; process-oriented; restless; makes decisions based on relationships/feelings; needs help in persevering; social butterfly.

Phlegmatic

Slow to react; doesn't react intensely; reactions of short duration; quiet; diplomatic; peaceful; makes decisions based on relationships/feelings; sensitive to others; dependable; procedural; dispassionate; dry wit; follower; introverted; calm under pressure; dutiful; likes structure; requires motivating; hates conflict; enjoys peace and quiet; well-liked by most everyone; peacemaker; reserved; homebody; constant; polite; prefers routine; process-oriented; patient; tolerant; not easily provoked, but feelings can be easily hurt; well-behaved; respectful; would rather please others than do what he wants; orderly; can be sluggish or indifferent; unmotivated; low-key.

∽

Biographical Note

Art Bennett is a licensed marriage and family therapist and director of the Alpha Omega Clinic and Consultation Centers, Catholic mental health clinics currently established in Maryland and Virginia. He is also the host and co-producer of *Healthy Minds/Healthy Souls*, a Catholic radio show in the Washington, D.C., area. He has more than twenty years' experience in the mental-health field and is a frequent speaker on marriage and family issues. He writes a monthly column for the *National Catholic Register*, on the topic of families and work.

Laraine Bennett has a master's degree in philosophy and is a freelance writer with articles published in *Faith & Family*, *Nazareth Journal*, the *New Oxford Review*, and the *National Catholic Register*.

Currently residing in Northern Virginia, the Bennetts have been married for twenty-eight years and have four children — one of each temperament type!

∽

Sophia Institute Press®

Sophia Institute® is a nonprofit institution that seeks to restore man's knowledge of eternal truth, including man's knowledge of his own nature, his relation to other persons, and his relation to God. Sophia Institute Press® serves this end in numerous ways: it publishes translations of foreign works to make them accessible to English-speaking readers; it brings out-of-print books back into print; and it publishes important new books that fulfill the ideals of Sophia Institute®. These books afford readers a rich source of the enduring wisdom of mankind.

Sophia Institute Press® makes these high-quality books available to the general public by using advanced technology and by soliciting donations to subsidize its publishing costs. Your generosity can help Sophia Institute Press® to provide the public with editions of works containing the enduring wisdom of the ages. Please send your tax-deductible contribution to the address below.

For your free catalog, call:
Toll-free: 1-800-888-9344

Sophia Institute Press® ◆ Box 5284 ◆ Manchester, NH 03108
www.sophiainstitute.com

Sophia Institute® is a tax-exempt institution as defined by the Internal Revenue Code, Section 501(c)(3). Tax I.D. 22-2548708.